Praise for *Making It Up*

"Christopher is onto something powerful. Some of my daughter's favorite childhood moments happened during unstructured playtime with her parents. Creating massive forts in the living room and pretending to stand up to bullies were highlights for my daughter."

—Tal Eyre, author of *Dad Mode: 25 Ways to Connect with Your Children*

"Joyful, uninterrupted play with your child allows for connection and belonging."

—Donna Tetreault, parenting journalist and author of *The CASTLE Method*

"When adults attend theatre, watch movies, and stream video series, they 'willingly suspend their disbelief' or 'agree to pretend' so that they can explore different worlds and live vicariously through characters played by actors. *Making It Up* provides ways for adults to give children that same lived-through experience of being somebody brave, bold, and adventurous in spectacular settings. Improvise with the children in your life and prepare to be awestruck by their creative characters and expanded language."

—Dr. Rosalind Flynn, head of theatre education at Catholic University

"Christopher's techniques will help you engage in play with your child in a way that builds imagination. Whether your kid dreams of fantastic dragons, silly adventures, or everyday activities, this book will help you find a way to connect and create stories together."

—Tracey West, *New York Times* bestselling author of over 200 childrens books, including the *Dragon Masters* series

MAKING IT UP

Published by Familius LLC, www.familius.com
PO Box 1130, Sanger, CA 93657

Familius books are available at special discounts for bulk purchases, whether for sales promotions or for family or corporate use. For more information, contact Familius Sales at orders@familius.com.

Library of Congress Control Number: 2025943765

Print ISBN 9798893960068
Ebook ISBN 9798893960891

Printed in China

Edited by Michele Robbins and Courtney Loi
Cover and book design by Brooke Jorden

10 9 8 7 6 5 4 3 2 1

First Edition

A Revolutionary Way to
Bond with Kids Through Play

CHRISTOPHER MANNINO

Illustrations by CORY REID

To Gavin and Gabby,
who taught me everything and more.

CONTENTS

SETTING THE STAGE

I darted past killer robots, leaped over a floor of flaming lava, and stood face-to-face with a ferocious dragon. Holding a sword that looked strangely similar to a cardboard tube, I stared at his glowing eyes. The dragon laughed. He was short for a beast, about the height of my son, actually. Flames licked his lips, and his wings flapped once. This wasn't good. I was late for my reservation at an extremely fancy restaurant. The kind that serves only the finest paper sandwiches, plastic oranges, and cans of beans. Yet, I had to complete this quest first. After all, I couldn't attend my date before retrieving what my kids had stolen:

My nose.

No, this isn't a cartoon or a fantasy novel. This is just *making it up*.

It's a daily thing now. Not every minute of every day, mind you. But the Making It Up Method has transformed my life and my relationship with my kids.

And it can transform your life too.

I recall a time when the sky was gray and my mood was grayer. It had been a rough day. A really rough day. I was tired, dejected, and just run down. As my six-year-old son Gavin approached the car, I knew at once that he'd had a similar day. Proverbial rainclouds hung over both of us—even inside the car. I didn't want rain on the upholstery or on my mood. Gavin sat, glum as ever. His three-year-old sister Gabby scrunched her face, readying a scream.

That's when the dragons first attacked.

It's a good thing I was driving, because I was able to swerve just out of reach of the oncoming fire blast and detour toward what I was going to suggest was the jungle.

"It's the mountains!" shouted Gavin.

Yep, it was the mountains. *Just say yes*, goes the first rule of improv.

The car behind us was likely confused. After all, they probably didn't see those mountains in suburban Delaware, which is laughably flat. They also probably missed the dragons overhead. But the car behind us didn't matter, because the indoor rain clouds dissipated, and sorrow turned to smiles. I used improv, some quick thinking, and intense listening. The tough moment had morphed into a good one.

I'm not alone in this type of parenting. Like many, I want to parent as well as I can. I want to be Bandit Heeler and Danny Tanner and Phil Dumphy rolled into one, even though I know they're all fictional. I want to be amazing.

It's not just me. You want to interact with kids better, and that's why you're here. The fact that you're reading this now is a great start. Good parents all want to be better. And not just parents, but *all* caregivers. You might not have kids at all. Maybe you're planning for a family. Well, put the order in from the internet and choose your shipping speed (or however it is babies are made these days). Maybe you're a teacher tired of herding cats. Wouldn't it be nice if the cats all behaved for a few hours? Whatever your situation, if you interact with kids, or plan to, this book is for *you*.

Let's go back to that quest for my nose. Seems unrealistic, doesn't it? Seems crazy. It's the type of thing you see on one of those YouTuber channels

with the people who look like they consumed a gallon of coffee before rolling the camera. Or an episode of *Bluey* where Mum and Dad are literally always animated.

Who parents like that? Who has the energy? Who has the time? Who has the skill?

Believe it or not:

You do.

Or you can, at least, with some guidance.

Let's also talk about the word *parent*. I use it a lot in this book. This is a parenting book, after all. And yet, as I mentioned, this guidebook will help *any* caregiver. If you're a grandparent looking to play better with your grandkids, read on. If you're a babysitter or nanny, this book's for you. Early childhood teacher or daycare worker? Yep, you too. If you want your interactions with children to be more meaningful and more authentic, I'll show you how.

But who am I?

Well, I'm a lava-crossing, dragon-fighting, nose-rescuing goofball. I'm a part-time robot, occasional spaceship, infrequent tree, and intermittent octopus. In other words: "Hi reader, I'm *Dad*."

Play-centered parenting is what every young child desires, yet it's hard to manage in today's hectic world. How can real-life parents with real responsibilities and stresses drop everything to be silly with their kids?

Don't worry, I'll show you. I've taught children and adults theatre for the past twenty years. It's easier than it sounds and far more powerful than you can imagine. This isn't just a book. It's a course with a set of tools that will transform playtime. Use these tools and discover more energy, more confidence, and a stronger relationship with your kids.

How?

By *Making It Up*.

. . . . .

The secret is improv.

Improvisational theatre, which is unscripted and unrehearsed, is the oldest form of theatre. It is arguably one of the oldest forms of communication. Caveman arrives back at the cave and instead of grunting or drawing about the mammoth he just killed, he starts acting out the hunt. Improv is an ancient, primal form of connection.

It's also the foundation for the Making It Up Method.

I need to pause a moment to repeat a sentence from earlier. Whatever your situation, if you interact with kids, or plan to, this book is for *you*. Yes, even if the words *improv* or *theatre* seem frightening. To many, the drama kids are those weirdos you avoided in high school. Maybe acting is something you'll watch in a movie, but it's never something you'd try yourself. And yes, this book is written by one of those weirdo drama kids who grew up to teach more drama kids. But don't worry. *You already have the skills to do improv*, you just don't realize it. Have you ever sat down at a "tea party" (or "coffee party" as mine prefer) with your kid and taken a "sip" of imaginary fluid? That's

Improv is an ancient, primal form of connection.

It's also the foundation for the Making It Up Method.

improv. Did you ever have a moment at work where someone did something completely unexpected, and instead of feeling annoyed, you just went along with it? That's improv. Improv is all around us in our lives, but this book will allow you to see the skills more clearly and refine them in a way that will revolutionize playtime. And all in **only ten minutes a day**.

I know it sounds too good to be true. Perhaps you're worried I'm making it up. Well, I'm not. But *you* will be.

. . . . .

When the pandemic struck, my son was suddenly home from preschool. The world had shut down, and we'd no idea when it would restart. Every routine and norm was thrown out the window as the world froze.

At first, panic surrounded me. This was some dystopian-level stuff, and very real fears consumed my wife and me as we were engulfed by bad news and more and more crazy things happening. My son was four. He didn't have the capacity to process the globe shuttering over a virus. He didn't understand why he couldn't see his friends. He couldn't fathom why mom and dad always seemed worried and stressed. And most of all, he needed us to be his rocks.

So, I improvised.

I literally *froze*.

As a theatre teacher, the game Freeze is what I always used to introduce my students to the skills of improv. It's a simple, foundational game. The TV show *Bluey*, which is highly based on improv, also starts with Freeze. The very first episode, "Magic Xylophone," is a game of Freeze the kids play with their dad. Freeze is always a great way to start improv.

You'll be doing Freeze with your kids later in the book, but I want to return to that moment at the pandemic's opening. As I stood frozen, unable to move anything except my eyes, my mind cleared. My son rushed to the other side of the room, grabbed a stability ball, and placed it in my lap. Then he grabbed some bead necklaces and hung them over my neck while giggling.

He ran to a bell and tapped it, effectively "unfreezing" me.

"What, how did I get these on me?" I started.

"Sillier," he demanded.

"I'm not silly," I responded, now in my spot-on Mickey Mouse falsetto. "I am soooo confused where this necklace came from, I just need a moment to get to the store, where I—"

"Freeze!" shouted my son.

The outside world was frozen and in fear. The norms were shattered. Yet, I was being reimagined as a goofball, and my son was calm and giggling. I'd improvised a reaction to one of the greatest stresses of our times and transformed the moment into intense playtime with my kid.

And through it all, I found my own stress vanishing. I had *fun*.

Yes, even in that moment so many remember with chills, I was enjoying myself.

This type of play might seem hard, but really it just requires a bit of training and practice.

Take another more recent example.

The pandemic was over. I stood in the grocery store with my then three-year-old daughter Gabby. Now that her older brother was back in school, shopping had become a daddy-daughter event. The store was moderately

crowded, and my daughter had a particularly three-year-old expression on her face. If you have ever had a three-year-old, you know the look I'm talking about. It's the calm before the storm, the bomb about to blow, and the dam about to burst.

The store was calm. Too calm.

And my daughter was planning to shatter that calm. It was time to kick into full-on dad mode.

I started as a robot. They're good at shopping. And it's easy to tie into actual productivity.

"Beep boop beep," I said in a monotone. Everyone who's played a robot knows that, despite the current year and the massive advances in cybernetics, all make-believe robots sound like clunkers from the 1980s. Heck, I'm a clunker from the '80s, myself, so can't go wrong, I suppose. I reached in full robot mode for the grapes and turned to my robot helper. "Do you want grapes, beep, beep?"

"No!" Gabby shouted, turning around. I hadn't hooked her. I saw at once the robot wasn't working. The hammer of her rage crept closer to the glass edges of the store's calm. She wound up an arm and reached out, grazing my elbow.

"Snowman?" I whispered.

A chill blew through the produce section as if Elsa had stepped out of Arendelle and was planning to belt out a Broadway showstopper.

Gabby's eyes shone. Like an actual gleaming-in-her-face glow. It was slight, and maybe I'm the only one who noticed it, but it was there. Her lips curled into a grin. That was all the acknowledgment I needed. Snowman it was.

I froze. Every fiber of my being tightened and constricted while I transformed into a snowman. Luckily my mouth wasn't completely iced over, so I could mumble slightly.

"Need heat," I half-said through clenched lips. I was mid-reach toward the apples. I couldn't move until I was melted, of course. But Gabby decided to bide her time.

None of the above was particularly unusual or unexpected for a shopping outing, but the next part really did surprise me. A woman walked up. My eyeballs were unfrozen, of course. No matter how frozen someone is, their eyeballs always remain free. Not sure why, but it's true. At any rate, a stranger walked up and smiled.

"You're a great dad," she said. And then she walked away.

A moment passed, and finally Gabby unfroze me by shining an imaginary heat ray in my direction. We continued shopping, rather haphazardly, as I kept becoming too frozen to put things in the cart. Shopping as a snowman isn't the easiest, but at least the frozen items don't thaw too quickly. We continued through the store, when yet another stranger approached.

"Well done, Dad," said this stranger.

What was happening? I'd been to this grocer hundreds of times. I'd sung aloud, played dozens of silly games there, and wasn't really doing anything different now. I'd honestly never really thought about the other shoppers. I mean, how could I? If I stopped to worry what everyone else thought about me, I'd probably never leave home. I suspect I'd be embarrassed and ashamed, at least if I was a different kind of parent.

But . . . I'm not embarrassed. Why should I be ashamed to play with my kids? Why shouldn't I play as crazy as I can? Why shouldn't I be a snowman or a robot? Playing with kids is *awesome.*

Here was the validation. Now that strangers were actually interacting with me and approaching me, they had only praise. They weren't laughing at me . . .

Wait, scratch that last one.

As we approached the coffee section and Gabby froze me a final time just inches from the espresso I wished was already brewed and pouring into my mouth, laughter broke the air. A child, probably five or so, pointed at me and laughed hysterically.

"We like silly dads," added his mom, as if I needed an apology of sorts.

Apology? What a strange idea. I'd never felt prouder.

That's improv energy.

The crazy thing is, once you embrace the improv and ditch the inhibitions, it's actually pretty easy. And super, super fun.

I've seen other parents at the store who push their kids in the cart and barely speak to them. They stare at their phones, read their shopping lists, and move in a daze. I'm not criticizing; parenting is often exhausting, and I've had a few shopping trips like that myself.

In fact, I'm often unsure if I'm a good parent at all. Every parent grapples with this self-doubt. You're reading this book right now because you want to be better. That alone means that *yes, you're a good parent.*

A good parent wants to improve. They know they don't have all the answers. After all, how could they?

. . . . .

Many things have training periods, requiring years of study and trial and error. Perhaps you worked for years to get where you are professionally or academically. Yet, there's no real "parent school" to teach you what to expect. There are books and trainings and tons of information out there, both good and bad. In fact, when you were first expecting your child, you likely heard from hundreds of people exactly what you should do and what you should expect. Everyone you know probably chimed in, whether asked or not, even those without kids. That's how it happened for my wife and me.

Funny thing is, while all those kernels of advice were well-intentioned, and many held some nuggets of truth, they were all wrong.

We were as prepared as possible to become parents.

And it was still completely unlike what we'd expected.

Seven years ago, the universe shifted.

The date will be different for each person reading, and maybe it hasn't happened for you yet. (Get ready, it's gonna be huge.)

I'm not talking about anything you read in the news. I'm talking about something far more important. This shift was the single biggest change possible. Galaxies flipped over, dark matter leaked into spacetime, and everything just sort of stopped.

Yeah, I'm talking about that crazy, tense, wonderful, exhausting, stressful moment when my first child was born.

You think you know what life's going to be like. You've read all the books and blogs and received advice from everyone you asked and at least a hundred people you didn't ask. You've prepared the crib and had a baby shower and have mentally told yourself that not much will change.

And then the baby comes.

All of a sudden, nothing in the universe is the same. You're not your own person in the same way, because you've just signed on for a new job, arguably the single most important job there is: parenting.

For the first few months, I was lost. I was treading water, at best. Parenting is exhausting work, and my wife and I did our best, but everything felt uphill.

The magic is *real*, and it's in your child's imagination, ready to embrace your own level of play.

Somehow, I transitioned from falling asleep on the floor, unable to remember my own name, and eventually ended up as the guy in the grocery store who would burst into character while people stared.

. . . . .

I'm a former actor, but there's no script for parenting.

And that's the beauty of it, right there. The secret to what I'm going to show you is actually the same thing actors use when they step on stage and don't know the lines.

That secret is *improvisational theatre*.

I'm going to walk you through the rules of improvisation and show you how to apply them to your own parenting. I'm going to show you that you don't need a cartoon or fantasy to embark on a magic-filled adventure. The magic is *real*, and it's in your child's imagination, ready to embrace your own level of play. I'll talk about the obstacles and the rough moments too. And I'll show you how to create that seemingly mystical energy that the best parents seem to always have. Hint: it's not just caffeine.

This book is step one on a journey with your kids.

Your worldview shattered when they were born. Now, hopefully, your approach to parenting will shatter once again. Play-based parenting can transform any caregiver/child relationship.

Just by *making it up*.

THE PROMISE OF YES, AND

What really struck me about the *yes, and* technique was that I already learned and had been practicing this as a Dungeon Master running Dungeons & Dragons games. Since my kids are the ultimate adventuring party for me, why not use those skills with them as well? My son sprung from around the corner with a bandana wrapped around his noggin and said, "I'm a ninja!"

I responded "I didn't hear anything . . ." to which he pancaked against the wall. Yes, you're a ninja, and you're very sneaky. Yes, I'm sneaky, and I'm currently hidden from view. We had both done *yes, and* with words and actions, and we were off on the quest together!

—Nathan Grajek, social worker and father of two, from Battle Creek, MI

It's gonna be different. And it's gonna be silly. But you'll be great.

You're likely reacting to that sentence with doubt. It's daunting to step outside your comfort zone. However, once you master improv, playtime really is magic. We're going to dive right into the rule at the heart of all improvisation—the promise that makes everything work.

The real tricky bit is that you've spent the bulk of your life being told to grow up. This is a truly unfortunate but necessary culturalization that involves learning rules and acting mature and all that other boring stuff. And yes, you'll eventually encourage your own kids to grow up a little too. But not today. Because today you're going to leave behind all the boring grown-up stuff and remember what it's like to be a kid.

Let's start with the promise that sets it in motion.

Think about that time I played freeze with my son. Like any parent, I had a choice. Play along, or don't. The easiest thing all parents learn is how to

The foundation to all improv, and everything else in this book, is that one ridiculously powerful word:

Yes.

say "no." Instinctually, you're doing it right from the beginning. "Don't chew that. Don't touch that. Don't do that." And a lot of those nos are necessary. Babies are ridiculous when they're born. I've never met a new human who didn't come with the self-destruct switch turned on and the instruction manual missing. Seriously, they'll put anything in their mouths and just jump off every ledge they see. Terrible initial design. Where can I leave a poor product review?

Still, once you grow accustomed to all the nos, one of the hardest words to say is "yes."

Yet, the foundation to all improv, and everything else in this book, is that one ridiculously powerful word:

Yes.

When Gabby turned me into a snowman at the supermarket. I had a choice. I could chuckle and keep shopping. I could say "I'm busy," or something to that effect. I could even give it a half-second acknowledgement before deciding it was silly and moving on. That's not what I did. I took the improv approach.

The first rule of improvisation is the most important. It's the one key that everything else depends on. And it's two simple words: "*Yes, and.*"

That's the rule. *Yes, and.*

The principle behind *yes, and* is simple, but the practice is hard.

Did I mention this whole chapter is devoted to just those two words?

It's true. Because countless parents and actors struggle with the concept.

. . . . .

Before becoming a stay-at-home dad, I taught high school theatre and coached an amazing improv team. They did fantastic shows, and got tons of laughs, but the moment that sticks with me most from all my years coaching them was one single rehearsal.

It was after school, and there were only nine people in the room: the eight kids on the main team, and me. No audience. No crowd. And for one glorious rehearsal, we dove into a long-form improv. This means that we built a play with no prompts, no scripts, and no practice. I improvised with them, and somehow, we told a coherent story with subplots and recurring characters that lasted about two hours.

We didn't know what would happen before we started. The lines weren't planned or rehearsed. Everything progressed spontaneously. At the beginning of the play, I was a server at a restaurant. Why? Because a kid sat down and asked for a menu. I immediately said *yes, and* to the suggestion. When I called another kid my son on the phone, he said *yes, and,* hopped right in, and then complained about his lost sibling. Didn't I miss them too? Of course, I did. I had to keep saying *yes, and.*

By the end, we'd rediscovered my son's lost sister, and embarked on an Indiana Jones–style quest for treasure, while meeting a scrupulous coffee thief along the way. The thief came back and eventually married my missing daughter.

The lines flowed, the scenes worked, and at the end, what I remember most was a feeling that we'd all worked together to create a true *story*, a true experience. It remains one of the highlights of my entire teaching experience, because even without an audience, we all turned to each other and said "Wow, that was amazing."

What had we done? What made this experience exemplary? We all said *yes, and* again and again. Like an entire film or novel, only without any planning or rehearsal or practice at all.

And that is what playtime should feel like with your kids too. Not every playtime is going to be an earth-shaking, life-altering moment. But some will. And the Making It Up Method will change you and your child for the better.

On the second day of lockdown, back in the COVID pandemic, my son started stacking pillows and chairs. "This is our rocket." *Yes, and* now we'll use it to fly to space. I accepted the premise and hopped in. I'll not lie, with the pandemic, I think we both had a subconscious wish to get as far away as possible. So, we did. We explored the solar system, visiting each of the planets one at a time. Even Pluto, because I grew up with it as a planet—and call me old-fashioned, but I felt like it deserved a stop too.

When Gavin asked if we could take a hitchhiker from Mercury to Mars, I wasn't going to argue. I said "yes," and we did.

We spent a long time on that expedition. We built off each other's ideas, and we made a song to remember the order of the planets. It was a wonderful, intense playtime that I treasured, and it helped dispel the fear settling over my family as the pandemic closed around us.

And it all centered on those two simple words:

yes, and.

. . . . .

Let's break them down.

Yes:

Yes, in this context, is the promise of acceptance. For many parents or caregivers, this is the most challenging step. Yet this is the moment that really decides it all. Accept the game, the reality, and the imagination. Or don't. That's the choice.

When you receive a piece of information, that information is *true*. It is the promise of the world. It is a new law.

For both parents and actors, this is far harder than it sounds. If your kid runs up to you, points a pencil like it's a wand, and tells you to fly, what are you going to do?

Most parents, realistically, say "no." This can take many forms such as "Oh, not right now," or "I'm busy," or "What are you doing?" It can even go so far as "I can't fly." If there is a negative response, that's it. Finito. That moment of potential playtime is over. The opportunity has been lost.

And here, we begin to see the true brilliance of improv. Because improv shows us what can happen if we instead say yes.

THE WAND POINTS. MAGIC IS REAL. SAY YES!

In one part of your brain, there's this unfortunate trap built by society and school and expectations and worst of all, adulthood. I say that last word with a shudder, as it's quite overrated. And that trap is quite simply a set of expectations for how the world does and does not work. One of those rules is that people don't fly. You know, gravity and physics, etc. Even Icarus fell, after all. Another rule is that your kid is always demanding something, or always taking energy. And isn't it easier to just say no? Or turn on the TV? Or turn away?

It's sad, but that mentality is so ingrained in most adults that they don't even see it.

Here's a trick to help you break free: Say yes.

Because your kid isn't encumbered by the same traps, expectations, or rules.

The wand points, and yes, it is definitely a wand, not a pencil. Yes, magic is real and always has been. He tells you to fly, and you know that he is a fifth-level mage who has trained at the finest wizard schools and possesses the power to command reality with a single word.

So you fly.

It doesn't matter how. Flap your arms. Maybe you become a bird. Maybe you even caw. Just try it. The hardest answer is actually the easiest to do. You've said yes to the kid's world. You've entered the improv. And you've started *creating* something.

The secret is *yes, and*.

Saying yes may be the hardest lesson in the book. And it's not just at the beginning of playtime either. Saying yes has to continue throughout playtime, and throughout an improvisation.

When teaching improv to high schoolers, I always began with a lesson on *yes, and*. I described the process like building a tower brick by brick. In a two-person scene, each idea is a brick. *Brick* is a term used to represent any concrete idea. A brick is essentially a promise or rule in the scene. These bricks become the foundation, and ultimately the walls, of a tower. When a brick is placed, the other actor has only three choices: they can knock that brick down, ignore the brick completely (which is a different form of saying no), or can *build on top of it*.

The secret is *yes, and.*

Guess what? It's the same when playing with kids. When they give you suggestions, or bricks, you have a choice of how to respond. You can deny, ignore, or accept the brick. Once you accept it, you move to the next step. You have to keep building.

And

Once you have an idea, you have to *add* to it. Only saying *yes* is a form of acceptance, but you won't be helping to build. And if you just keep saying yes to the bricks without adding, the kid is the only one participating. You aren't

playing with them, you're watching them.

Imagine Xaria and her mother. Xaria says she is a princess. Her mom says, "Okay." Xaria says, "It's time for a tea party." Her mom nods and accepts the cup of tea offered. Xaria then announces that it's time for cake. "Yay, cake," says her mom. Her mom's doing a great job of saying yes, but she hasn't said *and* once. *And* involves building. *And* involves taking an idea and adding another.

Xaria: I'm a princess

Mom: Your horse is ready, your majesty, I saddled it myself.

Xaria: You're a great horse-helper. You can have cake.

Notice that not only does Mom accept her daughter is a princess when she says "your majesty," but then Mom also adds a horse and her own role as a groom: "I saddled it myself." The differences might seem slight, but as the playtime progresses it's important to keep building—to keep saying not only *yes*, but *and. And* allows playtime to build and all to interact equally.

Here's another example of what *yes, and* looks like. Let's imagine playtime between Bob and his mother Jill.

Bob smiles at Jill and says, "Good evening, may I take your order?"

—Pause Scene—

Right away, Bob has laid down several bricks that the scene can build on. The first brick is time. It's evening. *This is now a law, or promise, in the scene.* If Jill responds by yawning and saying something about the beautiful morning, she's destroyed the scene, and it goes nowhere. The playtime is done.

Bob has also established their relationship. She is a customer and he is helping her. We don't know where exactly they are, but the relationship itself is concrete. And the wording seems to imply a restaurant.

Once Bob lays those bricks, Jill responds. There are countless ways for her to say no. In fact, she might have stepped into the scene with preconceived notions about what she wanted to show. Maybe she was planning to be a baby and wanted Bob to be her father. There's a tendency, especially among high school improv students, to try really hard to be funny. Yes, some people hear improv and think comedy clubs or *Whose Line is it Anyway?* Yes, improv can and will be funny, but it's never funny when you try to be. I'll come to that point in a lot more detail in chapter four. However, the problem comes right back to *yes, and*. If Jill ignores the bricks, the tower crumbles.

Instead, Jill decides to *accept* Bob's suggestions. Now comes the second part of *yes, and*. The "and." She accepts that she's a customer and that it's evening. Now she *adds* a brick of her own, building the tower slightly taller.

"I'd like to order a slice of pizza," Jill replies in a monotone. "Now that my upgrade is complete."

Excellent job, Jill. She accepted Bob's bricks. It *is* evening. She *is* a customer. She said *yes*. And then she continued by adding three bricks of her own. The restaurant serves pizza, she is an android or robot of some sort, and she's just been upgraded. Her bricks go neatly on top of Bob's bricks, and the scene progresses. She accepted the reality and she added to it. Who knows how high this tower can go? If they keep saying *yes, and* keep building, the scene can reach the sky. It could go on for two hours. Did I mention there are fully improved musicals each year in Washington DC? Yeah, even the songs are improvised. That's what a mastery of *yes, and* can lead to.

If you accept the reality presented—the bricks placed either by you or the child—you must then add to it.

This is the heart of the Making It Up Method.

If you accept the reality presented—the bricks placed either by you or the child—you must then add to it. Every idea, every brick, keeps the play going.

Similarly, every episode of *Bluey* works because in each episode, the family spends seven minutes continuing to say *yes, and* to each new idea. They take the promises of the game, accept them, and build upon them. In the episode "Bus" for instance, the family sets up the chairs. The chairs are a bus (brick). The two children, Bluey and Bingo, are grannies on their way to mahjong (brick). Their dad is the bus driver (brick). Their mom is a separate passenger secretly in love with the driver (brick). With every line in the seven-minute episode, a new brick is added, accepted, and built upon, from the steering wheel breaking off to the bus driver's rejection of the mother because he's already married to a giraffe. Line by line, the episode follows the course of an improv. It builds, brick by brick. And it's fun.

Adding a brick, or idea, to an improv keeps the scene building, keeps the play going, and frankly keeps things entertaining. The "and" in *yes, and* is just as important as the "yes". It ensures that everyone is participating, and everyone is playing equally.

Just to compare, here's the scene above if Jill says "yes," but doesn't say "and."

Bob: Good evening, may I take your order?

Jill: Sure.

Bob: Would you like a slice of pizza?

Jill: Okay.

Bob: And are you in fact the President? You look familiar.

Jill: Oh yes, I am.

You get the idea. In the above scene, Jill is saying yes. She's accepting Bob's bricks and ideas. And she's agreeing to the promises of the scene. However, she hasn't added any bricks of her own. Just like Xaria's mom earlier, saying yes alone is imbalanced. It isn't interacting in the deep way we want. By using *and*, the tower of bricks is getting higher and higher: she's the president, she wants pizza, etc., but the scene is off balance. In my classes, I used to refer to this as the "leaning tower problem." One person is trying hard to build a scene, but the other person isn't adding anything. Just saying *yes* is not enough. It always has to be *yes, and*.

This is especially important in the Making It Up Method. If you're not adding, the tower's not rising. The kid might be having fun, but it can be far more fun and more engaging for both parent and child to fully embrace the promise of *yes, and*. Conversely, if you're the only one adding ideas, and not listening to the kid, they're not having fun either. Both adult and kid have to work together equally in this.

It's worth noting that the kids won't understand the rules but you, the caregiver, do. This is covered in the next chapter. Also, there are extra considerations for special needs kids who might need you to interpret the rules a bit differently. I'll touch on those circumstances in Chapter Eleven.

What does it look like when both partners stick to *yes, and*...

Bob: Good evening, may I take your order?

Jill: I'd like to order a slice of pizza. Now that my upgrade is complete.

Bob: Oh, you're going to love the taste. I just upgraded last week.

The scene is building. It's getting more interesting each time someone says *yes, and*. Every time the promise of the play is accepted and built upon, the scene gets better.

Yes, these same techniques used in improv can revolutionize playtime.

. . . . .

It doesn't matter if you're an actor. You're the main player in the intense playtime that your child wants. You've already been cast, and this method is all you need. You're the star of this show. Keep saying *yes, and*.

The additional difficulty when playing with kids is that they're not necessarily going to follow the rules of improv, at least not all the time. They are pure fountains of creativity and are brimming with idea-bricks to build a scene. Yet, they don't necessarily know when to say *yes, and*. That's okay too, sometimes the parent just has to roll with it. You—the adult— are the true master of *yes, and*.

Let's go back to that day early in the pandemic when my son and I explored the solar system. It started when Gavin put two folding chairs next to each other and then arranged a group of pillows in front of them. To be honest, I thought this was going to be a fort of some kind. One of the hardest parts of improv is abandoning expectations. There's no script, no set plan. You will, quite literally, be making it up, so you need to be open to everything.

"Get in the rocket," Gavin said.

"Absolutely, Captain."

At once, I said *yes, and*.

Yes: these chairs and pillows were a rocket ship. It doesn't matter what I thought they'd be, what they look like, or what they could be instead. Gavin placed a brick into the scene and I accepted it.

And: I instantly added a second brick with the word "Captain." With that single word, I added another layer into the scene—our relationship. He was the captain. He was in charge. It wasn't clear if there would be more to our relationship than that, and that's fine. Remember a brick is a single idea, not a flood. I could have said something like, "Yes, Grandpa. I'll get in this rocket ship bound for Mars. We need to get you to the space rehab unit before the

Xyborgs free themselves from the curse you gave them." Yeah, I know how ridiculous that sounds, but trust me: I've heard worse as an improv coach. And I don't mean ridiculous in context. Xyborgs sound great. It's ridiculous that after one brick was added, someone would dump fifteen into a scene at once. That's not playing—it's bullying. As you start experimenting with these techniques, it is entirely natural to grab the reins and try to steer the play where you'd like.

As Elsa reminds us in song: "Let it go, let it go!"

Let go of all those anticipated plans, all those preconceived ideas, or even the attempts to force play to go a direction you expect. Because ultimately, as crazy as that Xyborg scene sounded, it was the comfortable, easy route I could've chosen. Comfortable for me, because I was in control of all the ideas. And if it's comfortable for me, it's misery for my kid.

Instead, stick with one brick at a time, and stick to *yes, and*.

"Get in the rocket," said Gavin.

"Absolutely, Captain."

We both climbed into the chairs, and started fastening our seatbelts. We were now saying *yes, and* not just with words, but with our *actions*. Obviously, a rocket has seatbelts, and we need to use them.

"Take us to the Moon," demanded Captain Gavin.

Yes, I'll admit I wish he'd asked me to set course with a proper bearing and engage impulse engines first. Maybe we need more *Star Trek* in our free time. Till then, I have to accept those bricks. Did you catch the two he added in that sentence?

By saying "Take us to the moon," he established that I was the pilot, and that we were headed to the moon. Those were two separate ideas, and I instantly accepted both. It was time for me to add two bricks of my own.

"I remind you, sir, that the new engines run on song." I said this, admittedly because in the back of my mind I didn't know how long I was going to homeschool, and I craved educational playtime. Teacher habit, perhaps. "If we sing about the planets, we can—"

"No, the engines started," he interrupted.

Gavin broke my brick. In fact, he broke two of them. The ship had new engines, and they only ran on song. Instead of saying *yes, and,* he instantly rejected those ideas. This is where it takes practice and skill. I cover the *guide* aspect of improv between parent and child a bit more in-depth in Chapter

Five, but one key is to never throw out a brick, even if your kid doesn't accept it the first time. Hang onto it in some fashion. With kids who don't realize how intensely they're playing, this technique of bringing ideas back can be especially powerful and meaningful.

In that moment, I had to say yes. Yes, clearly the engines were going. I shook my body and we zoomed into space. Yet, I had not forgotten those bricks I'd tried either.

I'll fast-forward to the conclusion of our time on the moon after we moon-bounced, collected samples, looked for life, and continued to say *yes, and* to each other.

"Where next?" Captain Gavin asked his trusty pilot.

"A space song will help me reprogram the engines," I replied, revisiting the rejected bricks from earlier. "Let's make up one together."

It took a few minutes and a pause to the holodeck (or the basement stairs) where a poster of the solar system happened to be hung. Yet, soon we were singing together:

"Around the sun, we have fun . . . Mercury, Venus, Earth, and Mars...but just you wait, we're not done . . . Jupiter, Saturn, Uranus, and Neptune . . . "

That song then became a brick in its own right. The ship reprogrammed to the sun, and we used the song we'd created as a guide for the rest of our exploration. Those rejected ideas hadn't just come back, they'd become the core of our playtime, and I'd managed to sneak in a bit of teaching too.

In fact, to this day, three years later, my son and I still sing the song we wrote in the heat of that moment. A song that revisited broken bricks from an improv. I honestly don't recall every detail of our playtime, but that song will always remain with us both. And how'd we do it?

By *making it up*.

It all comes down to just two simple words: *yes, and*.

Your turn.

Now that you know the trick, you're ready to reinvent playtime with your kids. If your son walks up and says "fly," try flapping your wings and adding what you're flying towards. If your daughter wants to track down a mysterious unicorn, strap on your unicorn-hunting gear.

Chances are, you've probably already experienced *yes, and* in playtime and didn't even realize it. The most common form is the tea party. Whenever either of my kids starts setting up a tea party, I'm fully onboard. I will pretend to drink from the cups and will cringe if the imaginary tea is too hot or if the plastic biscuits are too stale. Playtime isn't hard, this technique just allows you to take it further.

No, But

There's a counterpoint for *yes, and* that is only applicable to parents: *no, but.*

We're going to dive into this in depth later, but as you'll be trying it first-hand next chapter, I want to touch on the idea now. I also know the idea of nonstop *yes, and* is likely intimidating. So don't worry about nonstop; focus on ten minutes.

In reality, not every moment is the perfect time for intense play. We work, we have responsibilities, and we have lives. I am not saying to forget everything else all the time. That's unrealistic.

However, there does need to be some time when you are 100 percent focused on the child. This means no phones, no internet, no calls, no work, no distractions. All those things make for weak, unengaged play. The memes aren't going anywhere. The news can wait. Even the work emails can pause for ten minutes.

- No distractions, but only for a set time.
- Ten minutes is not a hard amount of time.
- Set a schedule. Post the time on the wall if your kids are old enough.
- Ten minutes of no interruptions.
- Turn the phones off, unplug the wifi, and turn off the TV. For real.

Ten minutes each day will not hurt your overall routine. And those ten minutes will be the most meaningful time possible with your kids. No, you won't necessarily be writing songs you recall years later (though you might). But you'll be listening *intently*.

That's the key to *yes, and*. Expectations cloud our minds, and only by allowing us to fully *listen* to what our kids say can we say yes to what they're suggesting. Your kid might be sending a brick at you, and you wouldn't even notice if you weren't ready to catch that brick, accept it, and start building.

Those ten minutes will be the most meaningful time possible with your kids.

It only takes ten minutes a day.

During those ten minutes, remember to keep saying *yes, and*.

Even if the kids throw a curveball with a few nos, redirect back to *yes, and.* Keep those broken bricks for later. The play will be intense. Start with a tea party and try building it. Are you actually a robot who's only just learned to taste? Where can your scene and playtime go?

Think this is all theoretical? Warning: the next chapter is the get off your butt and try it one. And yeah, it'll take some *no, but* as well.

- *No* interference. *No* phones. *No* distractions.
- *None.*
- *But* set a limit if needed. (Ten minutes is great.)
- *But* be careful when you schedule playtime.

It's okay to delay. If you're in the middle of a call and your kid comes up, tugs on your leg, and tells you that there's a dragon outside, you don't need to hang up to go strap on your armor. *But* you do need to assure them that you will have time to fight (or ride or befriend) that dragon later. Set a timer. Set a schedule. Do what you need to. But don't ignore the intense, no-distractions, play-based moments.

Ten minutes a day.

Start there. Say *yes, and.*

Then watch your relationships soar.

STUMBLING

I used the *yes, and* method after a rough day at school for my six-year-old son. He and his four-year-old sister swapped ownership of a restaurant, and I enjoyed a birthday cake with 777 candles on it (I'm very old, of course). When his sister got distracted by something Mom was doing, he and I received mail and discovered we were actually from New Zealand. We tried to fly there, found out the plane was missing parts, held a court case to arrest the bad guys who stole from the plane (my son was the judge), finally flew to New Zealand (he was also the pilot), nearly crashed the plane, and opened a new restaurant after we landed.

I got banana juice in my eye once—absolutely hilarious, turns out—then everything involved banana juice in my eye for a while. We nearly crashed the plane at least a dozen times. The doors fell open, and we were nearly sucked out another dozen times. Just roll with it! It's a game, right? It was fun and silly and exactly what was needed after a hard day at school. We'll definitely keep playing like this!

—Adam Jarvis, college professor and father of two, from Ottawa, Ontario

Remember when you bought this book? You likely thought it was just for reading. Well, hate to break it to you, but it's not. This is for *doing*. In fact, *Making It Up* is an entire *method*. As this chapter's going to start breaking into the getting-up-and-trying-it phase of the book, I want to add two very important notes:

1. **Anyone can do this. I mean it**. Yes, and that means *you*. Doesn't matter if you hate theatre, or hate being silly, or have never done anything like this. If you can commit ten minutes a day to trying this approach, your relationships will change. I promise.

2. **I recognize that some people might need extra help** Don't worry. Please visit me at www.ChristopherMannino.com/MIU.html for extra support. I have everything you'll need, from guide videos to tips and tricks. For those who want the most help, there is also coaching. I promise, *you* can do this too.

Let's also take a moment to look harder at *bricks*. I'm going to use that term a lot in this book, as it's one of the fundamental concepts. A brick is an idea you accept and build upon to strengthen play. Yet, recognizing bricks isn't going to necessarily happen all at once. That's why I'm going to clue you into the three main sources for bricks right now, and then have you try to find some yourself.

Brick Source One: The Kids

As far as ideas are concerned, kids are the initial source of bricks. Remember that you're coming up with bricks together. Yet, if you as an adult get stumped, just pause a moment and really *listen* to your kid. Just before sitting down to write this section, Gabby told me that it was Captain Green-Green's birthday. Captain Green-Green, it turned out, was a neon green highlighter, and he was Gabby's brick. This is not something I'd ever have planned or expected. These types of awesome suggestions are best when they start right from the little brick factories we call children.

Brick Source Two: The Environment

This is a bit of a cheat, but it's an important one. Everyone has the stumble moments. The so-called brain farts, where an idea won't come. You *want* to add a brick, but for the life of you, you can't think of one. Back to that example with Captain Green-Green the marker. I'd gladly jumped in to play along and lined up her marker friends at the marker birthday party. It's worth noting quickly that yes, improv-led play can involve using objects like toys, or even markers. It's still accepting bricks and building upon them together. The markers sang "Happy Birthday" of course, and then it was time for Green-Green to open her presents. As Gabby moved the marker around, mimicking unwrapping,

A brick is an idea you accept and build upon to strengthen play.

she paused. I could tell she wanted to suggest something but couldn't think of what to say. Then her eyes moved to the t-shirt I was wearing, which happened to be a Grogu (Baby Yoda from *Star Wars*) shirt. "Green-Green got a Grogu shirt," she announced. That's a brick right there.

Gabby demonstrated that when all else fails, grab a brick right from your environment. A noun, a verb, a relationship. There's *stuff* around us all the time. In just a moment, I'm going to give you some practice with this skill. But first . . .

Brick Source Three: The Back of this Book

Okay, this is an even bigger cheat than the one above, but hey, some people need the training wheels. Turn to the end of the book, and I've listed a few bricks to keep in mind should all else fail.

EXERCISE: FIND THE BRICKS

Okay, time for a quick exercise. Grab a piece of paper and a pen or pencil. Set a timer for five minutes. Write down what you see. Fill each of the sections below. You can also find a printable version of this (and other exercises) at https://www.christophermannino.com/miuresources.html

NOUNS/OBJECTS *example: chair or cat*	RELATIONSHIPS (FAMILIAL OR SPATIAL) *example: above or son*	ADJECTIVES *example: red or buzzing*
1.	1.	1.
2.	2.	2.
3.	3.	3.
4.	4.	4.
5.	5.	5.

After you've finished writing, check out your work. You have more than fifteen bricks there. Yes, each one works as a brick in its own right. Perhaps you wrote *buzzing* for an adjective or *cat* for a noun. Each of those can be used independently. They can also be combined to form different bricks. A *buzzing cat* (adjective plus noun) is far different than a cat or simply buzzing. It also opens ideas. Why is the cat buzzing? *Daughter* and *television* are both fine bricks, but put them together and you have a daughter television. Your daughter is a television? Isn't that instantly more interesting? And yes, add all three sections and get even more. Buzzing daughter television, perhaps?

Yes some of the bricks are going to sound a bit silly, but that doesn't matter. The point of the above exercise isn't even to use them, it's simply to illustrate that ideas are *everywhere*. It doesn't take a professional actor to use them either. In fact, you're soon going to be interacting with natural-born improv stars: children.

. . . . .

Ideas are *everywhere*.

I always loved the first week of school as a theatre teacher, especially when teaching kids who'd never taken a drama class before. These kids would stumble into class weary-faced, looking for their desks. But there were no desks in my room—no tables to hide behind. Within that first day, I'd have those kids on their feet, posing in frozen pictures called tableaux.

Why did I do this?

Because part of theatre involves leaving the comfort zone.

In a similar vein, it's time to leave the comfort zone of the cozy reader absorbing these words. It's time to move your body into frozen pictures. It's time to join in on the improv.

And the first game we'll try is freeze.

There's a reason Joe Brumm decided to use Freeze as the central game in his very first episode of *Bluey*. There's a reason versions of Freeze have been seen in countless other kids' cartoons. And of course, Freeze itself draws from playground games like Freeze Tag.

There are hundreds of variations of Freeze, but we're going to keep it simple and limit it to the style that's going to be easiest to learn and do with your kids.

IMPORTANT: THIS IS A CHAPTER OF STUMBLING AND MAKING MISTAKES.

That is okay! It's normal to feel silly. It's normal to forget a *yes, and* at some points or to try and take over a playtime or let the kid take over. It's normal to get frustrated when things don't go the way you planned. After all, we're just making it up as we go.

That's okay. After each time trying, I'm giving you some space to take notes on what worked and what didn't. In these early attempts, taking stock of how it went will be just as crucial as playtime itself.

Quick note: at this point in the book, all the directions will be centered as if there's just one kid. But what if you've more than one? What if you're a teacher with dozens? Don't worry. You should still start here, and if possible, try these approaches with a small group, or just one of your kids at a time. In chapter thirteen, I'll go a lot further into the different dynamics of multiple kids and bigger groups.

. . . . .

Ready?

Alright, it's time to play.

First, remember our *no, but* rules. No interruptions for ten minutes, *but* at a time that works for you.

Once you find a time that works for both you and your kid:

- No cell phone.
- No work.
- No TV.
- No distractions.
- Ten minutes. Set a timer if necessary.

Good, now let's review the biggest rule of improv, which we introduced in the last chapter.

Yes, and.

When ideas, also called bricks, are introduced to playtime, they must be accepted. And both adults and kids work together to build a scene:

- All bricks must be accepted.
- Say yes to every idea, and add your own.
- Don't hog the bricks — listen to the kid and add bricks yourself.

Let's start with the simplest form of Freeze. Simply freeze your body when the kid says to. Any type of trigger (freezing power) can work. You can use a magic xylophone like Bluey does, the word "freeze," or a completely different phrase or prop. For the first rounds, be sure it's the kid who does the freezing. This gives them a sense of control and power, and also gets you outside of your comfort zone.

"Freeze."

As soon as you hear the sound, you freeze. You can't move. And this is where that first *yes, and* comes into play. Don't cheat. Don't lean against a wall, looking at your phone. Seriously, I'm going to jump right out of this sentence and scold you if you try. Tense your muscles and make yourself frozen.

Yes, I am frozen, *and* you can position me. You're more of a mannequin than a statue. Let the kid move your arms. Let them put a toy in your hands. They'll be laughing now. The best thing you can do is to not laugh. The more serious you keep it, the funnier it actually is. Trust me.

Now, obviously, I can't tell you what will happen next. The beauty of improv is that there is no script or plan. But let's talk about how you react. For example, if the kid moves your arm and hands in a way that now shows your

fingers outstretched, you have to add a brick, or new idea, to the playtime. As soon as you're unfrozen, you can try to imagine that you're carrying a pizza box, or the engine to a spaceship, or a lost pirate treasure.

It doesn't matter what you add as long you add *something*.

Here's a quick diagram with some possibilities. It is important to note that these are NOT the answers about what you could do. The answer is that you should do something YOU feel is right. However, for some this is quite new, so this diagram can be your training wheels, so to speak:

POSITION MOVED TO	SUGGESTION ONE	SUGGESTION TWO
One leg/foot up	Stepping on an animal, perhaps a dinosaur	Just stepped on a pile of LEGOs
One hand out	Holding something very heavy, such as an elephant or spaceship	Holding a tray of food, such as a waiter might carry
Given a toy	The toy is a surprise gift for someone special	The toy is a phone you will use to "call"

POSITION MOVED TO	SUGGESTION ONE	SUGGESTION TWO
Given a new article of clothing, such as a hat	The clothes indicate a uniform, defining your profession: a fireman's hat for example	You are at a clothing store, trying on new clothes

This is just a small example of some of the countless ways your body might have changed by your kid before they unfreeze you. When the play moves on, either verbally or with an agreed-on signal, you must accept the kid's bricks instantly and your brick must be added on top. Then the play continues. Each time they freeze you, take it as a new brick and try to add a brick to go along with it.

For this first game, and first attempt at improv playtime, focus only on a few bricks at a time. In other words, the kid adds bricks by positioning you. You add bricks by accepting those motions and suggesting something to add on. If the kid plays along with your suggestions that's great, but if not, don't worry.

Every time they freeze you, think of the game as resetting from the beginning. We're back to no bricks at all.

Here's what it looks like broken down:

- Step 1: Kid says freeze.
- Step 2: Kid positions your body (adding a brick).
- Step 3: Kid unfreezes you, and you ACCEPT the position (*yes*).
- Step 4: You add a brick, by continuing to play in the new position (*and*).
- Step 5: Kid plays along, adding their own bricks, and you add more (*yes, and*).
- Step 5: Kid says freeze, and we return to Step 1 again.

It's all pretty straightforward.

NOTE: IF YOU'VE READ THIS FAR AND ARE NERVOUS ABOUT TRYING SOMETHING LIKE THIS YOURSELF, IT'S OKAY. IT'S OKAY TO FEEL SCARED OR SILLY OR UNCOMFORTABLE. FOR SOME, THIS SORT OF PLAY MIGHT COME EASILY. BUT FOR OTHERS, IT MIGHT FEEL FORCED OR ARTIFICIAL. STICK WITH IT, AND I PROMISE IT'S GOING TO BE

WORTHWHILE IN THE END. I CALLED THIS CHAPTER "STUMBLES" FOR A REASON. NO CHILD WALKS UNTIL THEY STUMBLE FIRST.

AND, AS YOU GO THROUGH THIS AND ALL THE FUTURE EXERCISES, KNOW THAT I HAVE VIDEOS WITH TIPS AND SOME COACHING OPTIONS AVAILABLE ON MY SITE WWW.CHRISTOPHERMANNINO.COM/MIU.HTML

Now that you've read through what this first playtime activity should look like, it's time to try. Set ten minutes to try a game of freeze. Feel free to explain the basic rule of freezing and unfreezing to the kid, but DO NOT try and explain bricks or adding ideas. In fact, as you go through the methods of improv in this book, it is imperative that you don't teach them to your kid. Your kid already knows many of the skills innately, as they're part of human nature. And by developing the skills of improv yourself, you will be more actively exploring a deeper playtime with your child by *doing* the work, rather than by trying to explain it.

REMEMBER: DO NOT TRY TO TEACH IMPROVISATION, OR BUILDING BRICKS, TO YOUR KID.

Ready to try?

Great.

After your ten minutes of playtime is up, come back to the book, or to a piece of paper, and jot down what happened. What went right? What went wrong? How did it feel?

WHAT HAPPENED?	WHAT WENT RIGHT?	WHAT WENT WRONG?
1.		
2.		
3.		
4.		

WHAT HAPPENED?	WHAT WENT RIGHT?	WHAT WENT WRONG?
5.		
6.		

I hope that Freeze was fun. In addition, hopefully you're starting to understand the power of bricks, and the importance of *yes, and*. Feel free to come back to Freeze as many times as you want to. It's a great and simple way to explore improv. In fact, if you stumbled a bit that first time, go back and play Freeze a few more times. Each play time should still be a full ten minutes of no interruptions, but make sure you've got the hang of this basic concept before moving on.

It's worth noting that the real power of the game lies in *listening* to the child, having them listen to you, and in repeatedly *accepting* each other. On the surface, it's just a silly game, but at its core, Freeze is a lesson in total mutual acceptance and respect, which is the bedrock for all good relationships.

Now, let's take playtime a step further. We're going to do one more game in this chapter, and we're going to set it at the most ubiquitous play space around: the tea party. Move over, Alice, we're all mad here.

First off, let's dispel the misconception that tea parties are only for little girls. Anyone can have a tea party. Make it a coffee party if need be or a dinosaur gathering or a Pokémon camp-out or whatever the age and likes of your particular kid dictate. For our example, we're going to stick with a tea party.

You do not need to do much to set up at all, but you should have a specific area. A table that's the correct height for your kid is usually best. Feel free to decorate or get out some tea party toys or arrange some other toys around the area (it doesn't have to be dolls—think action figures, animal toys, or whatever). All of this setup can happen *before* the ten minutes of playtime and does not have to be elaborate at all. Yet, the setup itself has become the first brick.

After creating a tea party area, let your kid take the lead. You can establish a brick with the setup, but then wait for them to establish exactly what type of social gathering is occurring. Are the dinos having a feast? Are the super heroes planning how to save the world? Whatever works, as long as it involves

a group of things around a single space.

Definition: tea party—noun: a group of things around a single space.

Okay, ready for the improvisation element?

Presetting a scene, such as a tea party, invites a jump-start into play.

You're going to be focused fully on *yes, and*. In fact, once the playtime starts, I want you to start every sentence with those two words. It might sound a little silly at times, but this will be another great practice at accepting bricks and building playtime together.

In freeze, we only built a row or two of bricks at a time, before resetting and starting fresh. Now, during the tea party, we are going to try ten minutes of continuous bricks.

Let me pause a moment to say two things:

First. Yes, you can do this.

Second. It's fine if a few bricks break, or even if you end up starting fresh midway through your first tea party. Don't forget: stumbles are fine.

Once playtime starts, serve the tea and listen. The kid will add bricks. Listen for what they say. Respond with *yes, and* at the beginning of every sentence.

Now, as before, I can't walk you through what to say. But again, here are some training wheels–style suggestions for things you could add.

PLEASE DO NOT LIMIT YOURSELVES TO THESE BRICK SUGGESTIONS!

IF THIS HAPPENS	TRY ADDING	OR ADDING
Tea is too cold	A dragon	An oven repairman
Tea is too hot	A blizzard	Ice cream
Cookies are out	A lonely chef	A gingerbread man
No one knows what to say	A dream vacation	An impossible quest

These are just a few ideas. Add your own. Improvise!

Remember, every time you speak, start with the words *yes, and*. It's fine if the kid starts talking this way too; many will, since kids are so naturally attuned to both improv and to copying adults.

Here's an example of how it might sound after setting up. Let's picture John and his daughter Katie.

Katie: Tea time!

John: Yes, and the peppermint tea is hot.

Katie: [Moving a doll.] I want hot cocoa.

John: [Picks up a different doll.] Yes, and your majesty's cocoa is here, upon this golden pillow.

Katie: I'm a princess?

John: Yes, and we are all loyal to your highness. Except for Robot Bob.

Katie: Where's Bob?

John: Yes, and we must find him! We must start a hunt . . .

This should give you a general idea. The words *yes, and* will not always fit naturally. But you, as the adult, must still start every sentence with that thought. Notice when Katie asked where Bob is, she accepted her dad's brick, and still added a brick of her own by suggesting Bob is missing. This was likely not her intent, but John is going to spin in that direction by focusing everything back to *yes, and*. At times it might sound odd, but if the play keeps

Nonverbal bricks are still bricks.

progressing, and you're genuinely listening to your kid, it should be intense and fun.

Now, there is the possibility that the kid isn't listening to you, or doesn't want to engage. Perhaps this is a new form of play for them. I will cover some of these issues in depth during chapters three to five, but for now just try your best. Remember: *any* idea is still a brick, and you still need to say *yes, and* to every brick. So, if you sit down and start serving tea, and he picks up a dinosaur and stomps around away from the table, he's still creating something. Accept that dinos stomp around the table and stomp right alongside with him. Nonverbal bricks are still bricks, as we saw in Freeze.

Let's break it down one final time for this second attempt at improv-led playtime:

- Step 1: Set up a tea party play area (before the ten minute play begins).
- Step 2: Listen closely to the kid. Any ideas they give are bricks.
- Step 3: Start your sentence with "Yes, and," then add something.
- Step 4: Repeat Steps Two and Three again and again until you're done!

One quick note of caution. In beginning improv, there's a common error of turning *yes, and* into a *no*. Make sure you genuinely accept the idea. If the kid says, "This ice cream tea is delicious," an adult might be tempted to say, "Yes, and it's not ice cream." Oof. They used the words *yes, and* but they didn't accept the brick, they smashed it. In fact, the response was one giant NO. When you come back to reflect on your playtime below, really take note of any times you said no. It's normal, especially when learning, but something to watch for and avoid as much as possible.

Now it's time to pause, set up your party, and play without interruptions for ten minutes. Have a great tea party, and then come back to reflect when you're done.

THEIR BRICKS	MY BRICKS	ACCIDENTAL NOs
1.		
2.		

THEIR BRICKS	MY BRICKS	ACCIDENTAL NOs
3.		
4.		
5.		
6.		
7.		
8.		
9.		
10.		

As you can see, I'd like you to try and identify the bricks that both you and your kid added. It might be way more than ten, but one brick a minute at minimum is a good baseline. Remember looking for bricks all around you at the beginning of the chapter? You know what a brick looks like. They're there.

Also think back to any accidental nos. That's okay, you're learning, and it's okay if the kid did too. At this point, I'm most interested in your recognizing when you said yes, and when you said no.

Remember, just like with freeze, the core of this game is about listening, mutual acceptance, and respect.

Also, just like freeze, feel free to come back to the skills in *yes, and* as many times as you need. In fact, if you've been playing with your kid for years and just can't think of anything to say, repeat those two magic words: *yes, and.*

Of course, *yes, and* isn't the only rule. If you're ready, let's learn some new ones.

RULES

When adults attend theatre, watch movies, and stream video series, they willingly suspend their disbelief or agree to pretend so that they can explore different worlds and live vicariously through characters played by actors. *Making It Up* provides ways for adults to give children that same lived-through experience of being somebody brave, bold, and adventurous in spectacular settings. Improvise with the children in your life and prepare to be awestruck by their creative characters and expanded language.

—Dr. Rosalind Flynn, head of theatre education at Catholic University

Kids are natural brick builders, in terms of improv. One reason I encourage you not to teach the structured rules to them is that many kids will be doing them innately, and trying to add details could actually hinder their play.

In December 2023, following a week of being ill, I lost my voice. I'm a loud person naturally. A singer, actor, performer, and general loudmouth. And my voice stopped working completely. For several days, I couldn't get my vocal cords to move, not even a little. Needless to say, playtime with the kids wasn't what I or they were used to. All of a sudden, my entire communication strategy had been tossed out the window.

I sat with Gabby at the kitchen table, and she picked up a small toy, moving it around.

Gabby, as the toy, said "I need to go home. I need my house."

I wasn't feeling the best, so didn't feel like getting up, but I still wanted to play. So, without really thinking, I cupped my hand on the table. Remember, I couldn't talk or explain that this little arrangement of fingers was a not-great attempt at a house for the toy.

Bricks don't need to be verbal to be understood.

Gabby, aged four at the time, didn't miss a beat. She moved her toy under my hand and said, "I'm home." Without any hesitation, she accepted my brick—that my hand represented the figure's home—and then she instantly added a brick of her own. "Mom's coming."

I moved a finger on my other hand. Realizing I couldn't talk, Gabby pointed and stated, "Mom." Another brick. That finger on my right hand was Mom. My left hand was the house. Even without vocal communication, we were setting bricks and building intense playtime.

How? By showing me characters and making choices. This is similar to the tea party setup. An arrangement of objects becomes a brick. Or an action or pose can become a brick.

Think about this for a moment. You already know many poses that instantly show bricks. For example, imagine one person gets on one knee and holds a ring up. No words, but instant relationship and expectations. Or one person puts imaginary handcuffs on another. Again, no words, but instant relationship. Bricks don't need to be verbal to be understood.

Remember, kids are natural bricklayers. You can be a natural too.

By now, you are hopefully starting to grasp *yes, and* which is the core of all improvisational-based play. You know how to spot bricks and how to accept them. And you've hopefully had some great new playtimes with your kids, perhaps a bit more intense than you're used to. If all is going well, you've also realized the power of those daily ten interruption-free minutes as well.

Well, now let's add a bit more. Let's dive into some of the other rules and strategies from improv and show you how a deeper understanding of these techniques can transform your interactions with children.

Quick note. If any of this starts seeming overwhelming, or you need some videos to walk you through what I mean, be sure to look for the full range of video supports at https://www.ChristopherMannino.com/MIUresources.html.

I WANT TO EMPHASIZE: THIS IS FOR EVERYONE. YOU CAN DO THIS.

Alright, now let's add some important rules to the playtime.

Keep Adding

Okay, with *yes, and,* we learned to add. But it's important to keep adding. In fact, for beginners, remembering to keep going and keep building for the entire playtime can be one of the biggest challenges.

In short, it's easy in intensive play to forget to play along. Kids are definitely natural bricklayers. And the easiest thing to do when playing with them is to let them have the fun, while you watch.

It's worth noting, this isn't bad, in itself. In fact, child-led play is the basis for many types of therapy, including Parent-Child Interactive Therapy (more on that in chapter five). But, for us, it's also not ideal.

In the lens of improv, when you start a scene and only one person's adding bricks, the scene quickly collapses. Think back to those examples in the last chapter where one person added brick after brick, contributing idea after idea, and the other didn't add anything new. This type of play is one-sided and static. From a psychological point of view, you're not getting on their level. You're watching them play, without playing *with* them.

Let's put this really simply: your kid *wants* you to play with them.

Go back to the ubiquitous tea party. Your kid doesn't just want you to sit and say yes, as they pour imaginary tea. Your kid wants you to ask for sugar, spill a bit of tea by mistake, and praise the brew. Your kids wants *more*. For ten minutes a day, you're going to give it to them.

Keep adding.

Remember that "find the bricks" activity from last chapter? If you're stuck, use your eyes and ears. There's something right in front of you, which is in fact a brick.

Gabby walked up to me one day and said, "Sit down, this is school."

I immediately sat. *Yes.*

"I forgot my lunch today," I said in a little-kid whiny voice.

She spun, looking at the coats poking from the closet. "I'll get Mrs. Coat," she replied, marching off.

She said *yes, and*—and leaned into a quick-grab brick of the first thing she saw.

JUST. KEEP. ADDING.

Avoid Questions

Depending on how old your kid is, you might hear questions a lot, especially "why?" There's a natural phase of development where the word "why" seems to be all your kid can say in response to . . . well, everything!

"Time to get dressed."

"Why?"

"You need to go to school."

"Why?"

"Because it's Monday."

"Why?"

"Because since Ancient Babylonian times, we've associated the second day of the week with the moon. In Old English it was called *Mōnandæg*, which eventually evolved into Monday, and that is the day it is today." [Voice gets louder, sharper.] "You go to school because mandatory schooling has been an American benchmark since the Puritan times. And because I said you have to go to school and get dressed!"

Alright, admittedly your conversations might not go exactly like the one above, but do you notice the error in the conversation from an improvisation standpoint? Do you see the reason it's annoying to constantly hear "why?"

Simply put, asking questions is like skipping a turn. Bob lays a brick. Gina asks a question. In doing so, she *adds nothing* and waits until Bob lays another brick. Gina then asks another question, again skipping her turn to contribute. Bob lays brick after brick by himself.

ASKING QUESTIONS ADDS NOTHING TO THE PLAY.

This is tied to the rule we just mentioned: questioning isn't adding.

Now your kid will ask questions. That's normal and fine. However, during those ten minutes of intense play, I want you, the adult, to refrain from questions as much as possible. Every time you ask a question, you're asking the kid to add something extra to the playtime, instead of suggesting and adding something yourself. And the longer you go without questions, the less questions they'll ask too.

IN GENERAL, QUESTIONS DODGE BRICKS. AVOID THEM.

Here's an example of how this might look when done correctly. In the following example, Don is an adult and Brian is a kid. As you read, watch how Don refrains from questions, so he can continue adding bricks. Brian, especially at the beginning, asks many, but soon picks up on Don's cues.

Don: Watch out for dragons!

Brian: What? Where?

Don: Behind you! Duck! [Rolls on floor.] Take this sword.

Brian: Is this a sword?

Don: Yes, my king, I am proud to carry your sword for you when needed.

Brian: My sword is magic!

Don: Look at that! The magic sent the dragons far away.

Brian: Now we can feast!

Don: I'm opening the mead now, my king.

Playtime won't always go smoothly. And of course, the kid might take longer to stop asking questions. But in the example above, notice that every time

Bringing "lost" bricks back is true improv mastery.

a question was posed by the child, and no bricks were added, the adult still said *yes, and* while continuing to offer bricks. Also, recall that the words "yes, and" don't have to be used every time to say them.

"My sword is magic" was the first brick suggested by Brian.

"Look at that! The magic sent the dragons far away." Don said *yes* the sword is magic, *and* it transported them.

Every time a question was posed, the adult pushed the scene forward. If you want another example and are a fan of *Bluey*, go watch the episode "Work" from Season One. It's a perfect example of a continuous improv with a parent as guide (see Chapter Five for more on this), ignoring the missed bricks from the kid. In fact, in that episode, Bluey even goes so far as to negate a few bricks that Dad suggests, only to have Dad bring them back later. Bringing "lost" bricks back is true improv mastery.

As you approach intense playtime daily and are mentally preparing for the *yes, and* interactions, remind yourself to avoid questions.

Note: There's a loophole. You can technically add while asking a question. And once you get really good at this intense playtime, you'll see how. But for now, trust me, don't ask questions.

Don't Break the Bricks!

This is a bit different than everything before.

- Remember, bricks are ideas.
- Don't break the bricks.

There are two parts to this. On the one hand, don't destroy something that was given. Remember *yes, and*. Breaking a brick is just a fancy way of saying *no*.

Here's a terrible playtime of broken bricks:

Kid: This is my rocket.

Jackie: No it isn't.

Kid: And it flies to Mars.

Jackie: That's just a chair, honey.

Kid: I'm on Mars now, and the alien's coming.

Jackie: I don't see anyone coming.

Look, we've *all* been there. We are all Jackie. We've all had playtimes that look something like that session above. I certainly have had them. I've had days where I do not play my best with my kids. Yet, let's forget those playtimes, and focus on the new ones. Let's build together.

Notice in the above example, every time the kid laid a brick, the mother smashed it. Not only did she not say yes, but she downright said no. "That's just a chair" is a variant of a line every parent, including me, has used at some point.

The kid sees a rocket, but your mind is on work and your spouse and that meal you're trying to cook, not to mention the taxes are due and the toilet is clogged and did you see the news and on and on . . . . In that moment, you're not ready to engage fully with playtime.

Don't forget it's okay to set boundaries. It's okay to say, "not now, but soon." As long as you get to those ten minutes at some point each day.

When you are in that ten-minute period, that's when bricks are real. They're unbreakable, permanent ideas. And when the kid lays them, you lay your own right on top.

Kid: This is my rocket.

Jackie: As a rocket certification expert, I deem it fit to fly.

Kid: And it flies to Mars.

Jackie: Look at it go! I'm so proud of my sister and the rocket she built.

Kid: I'm on Mars now, and the alien's coming.

Jackie: [Pretending to be on phone.] Sister, it's me! I just heard the aliens are on Mars, look out! The only thing they want is pizza.

Same scene, but now Jackie's ready for it. She's fully engaged for ten minutes, no phones (aside from a pretend call), no worries, no work, and no news. Yes, it's hard to mentally disconnect, but it's actually great for you too! And the work, spouse, cooking, news, etc. won't be changed by ten measly minutes. Your relationship with your kid, on the other hand, *will.*

DON'T BREAK THE BRICKS.

There's another layer to this rule.

Bricks are *permanent.* At least as far as those ten minutes go. This is a tricky one for a lot of people who are new to this method. Maybe it's easy enough to acknowledge an idea and add. Yet, that idea also remains. It remains for those ten minutes.

In other words, if the chair's a rocket at the beginning of playtime, it's a rocket for the rest of playtime. Don't sit on it like it's a horse. Similarly, if you've called your kid your sister, she's your sister. For those ten minutes. The relationship sticks. Every brick you've added sticks.

Don't forget the metaphor of building upwards. It's the single metaphor we keep going back to. You can't build if you keep breaking bricks.

DON'T BREAK THE BRICKS!

And there's another caveat: What if the *kid* breaks the bricks?

This may come as a complete shock (he states in a thoroughly sarcastic tone), but kids change their minds. Yeah, the kid said they wanted an apple. Why are they crying when you put an apple in front of them? Yeah, those same kids.

Here's the secret, the key that makes this method so revolutionary: If you as the adult guide follow these rules, the kids start picking up on them. The longer you keep building, by adding and adding, refraining from questions, and not breaking any bricks, the better the kids get at it too. They're natural sponges and born improvisers.

Keep at it. And keep going.

Remember that *Bluey* episode "Work" I mentioned? I love watching Bandit's reaction when Bluey smashes some of his bricks early on. He pivots instantly, but knows the bricks are permanent, and brings them back later. It's a genius, master-level move. And the kind you'll be making soon enough.

The first three new rules:

- Keep Adding.
- No Questions.
- Don't Break the Bricks.

. . . . .

All right, time for some practice on those new rules. It's a lot to take in. So, bookmark this page, and get ready to play with your kid.

As you do, remember to have fun. Yes, there are lots of tips and tricks. Lots of new rules to consider. Yet, having fun is still at the core of this intense playtime between you and your child.

After you're done, come back and complete the table below.

- Do not write in this while playing.
- No distractions.

You set the limits of when you're available, but when you're with the kid, there's nothing else.

Think about your playtime. What bricks did the kids add? What about you? You should be able to easily come up with ten for each. Now, did any rules get broken by you? Don't worry or think about any that the kid might have broken, that's not important. Did you, the adult, break any bricks? Did you forget to keep adding? Maybe you asked a few questions, putting the focus on them? Go ahead and mark it.

And when you play again, do a little bit better.

THEIR BRICKS	MY BRICKS	RULE BREAKS BY ADULT
1.		
2.		
3.		
4.		
5.		
6.		
7.		
8.		
9.		
10.		

When Gavin was three, we went for a walk in the woods. It was a sunny spring day—the kind of brisk but gentle air that makes you glad to be outdoors after a long, dreary winter. We stopped just past an overturned log and I froze, my entire body rigid, staring at the ground.

"Dragon prints," said Gavin.

I'd added a brick, just with my body language. We hadn't been in playtime, and weren't in the house, yet the opportunities for intense improv-based play are endless. Gavin, a natural improviser, accepted my brick (that there was something interesting and unusual there) and instantly added to it (now, there are dragon prints).

"Look there." I pointed to the trees behind us. "There are branches broken where they flew."

"I see a dragon in the distance!" He pointed the opposite way.

"Shhh!" I quickly lowered to the ground, raising an imaginary shield. "They've got powerful hearing."

"We need a wand to get them!"

Well, this went on for some time. Yes, you can see he takes after his fantasy writer of a dad. But more than that, it's a good example of following those new rules. Every moment, we kept adding. We accepted our bricks without breaking any, and we avoided questions. Think of how it easy it would've been to ask "Where?" when he mentioned dragons in the distance. Yet, the question wouldn't have added anything. That would've skipped my moment of play and made him come up with more. I have to keep adding, not just watch. Note that Gavin's nonverbal crouch to the ground added a brick of its own.

Not every Making It Up playtime is going to be perfect. There are going to be stumbles and bumps. But if you commit to ten minutes daily, you're going to master these skills fast, and your playtimes will change dramatically.

Need a quick reminder or brain break? Go watch a few episodes of *Bluey*. Every episode is based off a different improv game, or a different session of improv-based play. Pay attention to the bricks and the way they build the momentum. Watch how even if the kids break a brick (rare, but sometimes happens depending on the episode), the parents do not.

One fun episode to try of that show is the episode "Octopus." It's about a dad who wants to do improv with his kids but can't. He's not one of the main characters, but the father of a friend. And throughout the first half of the episode, he breaks bricks by constantly saying no. When he and his daughter realize their problem, they both switch to saying *yes, and*—now the play can progress. It's a perfect example, in a seven-minute cartoon, of the power of these improv rules.

Stay in the Moment

The fourth rule is essentially *carpe diem*. When you're in intense playtime, you must be there, in the present. Seize every moment of it. We've talked a lot about ignoring all the other background noise. Work, spouse, house, pets, climate change, politics . . . none of that stuff matters during those ten minutes a day. Only the kid and the playtime matter.

Yet, this rule also digs a bit deeper. Remember, we're adding bricks to build a strong foundation for play. If you've ever played Minecraft (or seen a kid play it), think about the way you make a house. You place a brick, one at a time, on top of each other. Now, imagine you're in that same game of Minecraft, but after putting five bricks in a row, you start adding bricks randomly in other places far from those initial ones. Nothing's getting built. Even though you're technically adding, you're not focused in the right direction.

In terms of play, this means that you want to add bricks about what's happening *now* and with the people right there.

Remember Gavin and me following the dragon footprints? When he decided they were dragon footprints, I could've mentioned that they were made a thousand years ago, and then talked about where the dragons went. Perhaps they flew to a mountain in the sky. Now he wants to know about that mountain . . . and we're not playing. We're storytelling, which is fun, but we're not *in* the scene.

Instead, we remained focused on a dragon right there that was an immediate threat. The evidence was stuff right around us that we could see and interact with.

In a similar vein, avoid talking about stuff "offstage" so to speak.

Katrina walks up to her mom, holding a teapot.

Mom looks at the teapot, trying to add, and starts discussing buying it with her now-deceased grandmother. To be fair, that's a brick, and she is adding, but she's not staying in the now. Katrina can continue hearing or even asking about her great-grandmother, but there's nothing building in *this* scene. Instead, they're describing another scene. They've placed that Minecraft brick a mile from the ones they're near.

Be Specific

I've said many times now that bricks are ideas. But a lot of ideas are really big, nebulous things. For the play to work, focus on the most *specific* bricks possible. The more specific, the clearer the playtime. And remember, these are kids. If you're going to sit down at a tea party and announce that you are the physical embodiment of ennui or the personification of capitalism, you're going to get some frowns and odd looks.

Specific doesn't always mean simpler. For playtime, it's better to add extra bricks than to forget to add enough. The strongest bricks contain multiple, specific elements. Think back to that find the bricks activity. "Daughter" wasn't as specific as "daughter television" which in turn wasn't as specific as "buzzing daughter television." No, I'm not talking about a girl who watches TV. I'm saying that your daughter is a television, and is now buzzing. Yeah, it sounds weird, but it's also the specifics that give the Making It Up Method its most fun elements and its uniquely creative structure.

Here's a quick rundown of added specifics to tweak some common bricks:

INSTEAD OF	TRY ...
The tea is hot.	I burned my lips on this tea, and need ointment.
That's my son.	That's the son I haven't seen in five years.

INSTEAD OF	TRY ...
I'll buy that thing there.	A magic harp! I need to buy one to save my father.
The wind blew.	Brrr. That cold wind feels like a storm's coming.
Take this.	Take this key, and use it to unlock the silver door.
Wow.	I am happy to see you standing after the accident.

These are generic examples. But hopefully, you see that the column on the left is technically adding bricks, but the bricks are weak. They need more. "Wow" isn't much of a brick, to be fair. But saying "take this" is. You're giving something, you want them to take it. A bit of specificity makes a world of difference. Take this key and unlock a silver door. I'll bet there are some fun specific bricks coming after that!

Toys: They Aren't Necessarily Your Friends

Okay, sooner or later we need to address the elephant in the room. I'm talking about the gray plastic guy over there on the floor, beside a pink dinosaur, a collection of various action figures, and a blue truck. Yes, I'm talking about toys.

Until now, I've focused on playtime without mentioning the use of toys at all. In the theatre biz, we call these props. But in playtime, toys are a bit different. Toys can be wondrous windows into new realms of imagination and creativity. But they can also have issues.

There are two main types of toys: ambiguous and specific. Basically, anything that tells you what it is supposed to be is what I call a specific toy. That Batman action figure? Specific. The set of *Paw Patrol* toys? Specific. Your action-packed working Buzz Lightyear? Yeah, you get the idea. Super specific.

At the same time, there are very ambiguous toys. That elephant in the room might be just that: some elephant. Even more ambiguous are things like building blocks or dominoes. For improv-based play, the *less* specific the toy the better.

Wait a minute. Didn't I tell you just one rule earlier that specific is best? Yes, I did. But there's a catch. The specificity you want comes from you and the kid. It comes naturally from the scene. That can be tricky with toys. For example, let's say your kid picks up a Superman figure. He wants to play with it in the playtime.

Instead of a blank slate that you can build off, you're dumping a ton of bricks at once. Superman, Clark Kent, kryptonite, flying, superpowers, the entire backstory is there before you've said a word. Play acting with toys can be great, but it's not quite as involved as the type of intense improv-based play I'm advocating for. It's also better to try and use your body in the playtime, if possible. *You* being Superman is going to be a lot more meaningful to your kid than you manipulating an action figure.

That's not to say that improv-based play with toys or props is impossible. In the film *Toy Story 3*, there's a moment when Woody awakens in an unfamiliar room. A child he doesn't know starts acting out a funny scene. Woody doesn't know where he is, and one of the other toys, unsure of his own setting,

The key to playtime is you and the kid.

responds, “We do a lot of improv here.”

Yes, toy-based improv is possible.

First and foremost, the toys do *not* have to be what you thought. I’ve had a boss who happened to be a marker. I’ve fought dragons holding what appeared to be a Curious George doll, but was in fact a magic, shapeshifting sword. I’ve seen elephants fly and houses talk. You get the idea.

If you’re going to use toys, be prepared to think *outside* the package. Look beyond the label. Honestly, if it’s a toy that makes noises and repeats catch phrases, it’s not ideal for this sort of play. That spiffy light-and-sound Buzz Lightyear can pretend to be other things in the film, but in playtime, he’s pre-programmed with a few catch phrases that are hard to work around.

Things that do work well with toys are often environments where other things might be found. A zoo, for example, or a factory or circus. If you need a crowd, feel free to use some toys and other props. Just remember that the key to playtime is you and the kid.

The minute playtime becomes more about the toys and less about the people is the moment you’re no longer in deep improv-based play. That’s back to storytelling. You’re telling Superman’s story. Maybe it’s the time he rescued Baby Shark from Iron Man, Mr. Potato Head, and Pikachu. It’s fun, but it’s still someone else’s story. We want *your* story. You need to be in there, doing the rescuing to achieve that true connection we’re going for.

Don’t Plan Ahead

This is a core tenet of improvisation. It’s a rule all of my theatre students struggled with. And as both theatre and life go, it’s a bit counterintuitive. After all, what is this book you’re reading? In a way, isn’t it one big plan?

Guilty as charged.

Many people are natural planners. Whether it’s a grocery list before shopping, a to-do list at home, or a simple mental image of what’s coming next, we like to predict the future. Entire careers (meteorologist, stockbroker, etc.) are based on making a living guessing what’s coming down the road. As a writer, I outline before I sit down to draft. And as an actor, I love a script in my hand. It tells me what I’m going to say next, and what everyone else is going to say as well.

Yet, improv is different.

There's no outline. No script. No to-do list. No forecast. No plan.

The only way to truly succeed at the Making It Up Method is to embrace this element of improv wholeheartedly. You *cannot* plan ahead.

Why?

Because plans fail. And plans lead to broken bricks.

Imagine Rob walks into playtime. He's excited to join his daughter Kelly in some intense improv-based experiences. He's been thinking about this for a while now and has it all figured out. He's going to be a king, and she's going to be the princess. He'll move a chair to be the castle, and he's going to let her stand on it like she's in a tower. Oh, this is going to be so much fun.

Playtime starts, and Kelly looks up at Rob. "A robot teacher today, wow!"

Rob is frozen, unable to think or move. He's not supposed to be a robot or a teacher! This isn't what he planned at all.

Nothing bad happened in the scene, but something really tricky happened in Rob's head. I can't tell you how many times I've seen this. Even improv professionals occasionally fall into this dangerous trap. It's a tricky one, because planning is so natural to many of us.

DON'T PLAN AHEAD.

Rob didn't actually break any bricks. Neither did Kelly. Yet, by stacking up bricks in his mind, Rob was completely unprepared for the great bricks Kelly added. He wasn't in the headspace to actually engage in improv-based play. You can't *make it up* if you plan ahead.

Planning *never* works, because you never know what brick is coming next. That's the challenge and the beauty of improv. If you can abandon the plan, you'll have fun.

Go Big

This is our final rule for the improv focus of the Making It Up Method. There's plenty of other nuance, but think about the best times you've had with your kids. The times you felt most connected. Chances are you were going *big*.

You can't *make it up* if you plan ahead.

Everyone has a comfort zone. It's how we work. Some of us have a comfort zone that's a bit closer in than others, but that's not important. As you're reading, take a moment to visualize your comfort zone. Imagine a white line around your body. It's there, a physical separation from what you like to do and what you *could* do if you stepped a bit further. And with this next rule, I want you to *cross that line.*

Improv doesn't need to be silly. *Whose Line Is It Anyway?* and similar stage shows make money off of improv as comedy. Yet, improv as a skill isn't about comedy—it's about building. Adding bricks to create meaningful structures. The structures we're focused on, of course, are intense playtimes. When you're building those playtimes, and I ask you to step outside your comfort zone, the first impulse is to go silly. That's not bad, but it's not the only way.

Go big.

What does that mean?

It means that I want you to throw yourself as fully into play as possible. If you're flying to the moon, use your whole body. Extend your arms, shake, use different voices. The more you do, the more *connection* you're creating with your kids.

Go big means I want you to try and see the world through the kid's eyes. For some, this is way outside of their comfort zone. Saying *yes, and* is tough for a lot of people. Using your full body, or a silly voice, is an entirely new level.

Yet, at its core, this rule is the simplest to understand. So go big for ten minutes a day, that's it. That's all I'm asking you to devote to this method. It's not much, so you have to make every second of those ten minutes count. Before you read this book, your kid might've looked at you and said you're a robot. You might've smiled and said sure, and not responded further.

But you know better now. Full jerky motions. Robot voice. Freezing if you're low on oil. You're in this to win it. So go big!

. . . . .

All right, that's your tool kit. Let's review. We now have ten rules:

1. ***Yes, and*** is a great place to start. Accept the ideas (bricks) and add to them.
2. ***No, but*** allows you to pick when you'd play, but during those ten minutes, you have no distractions.
3. **Keep adding.** Keep going, and keep contributing to the playtime.

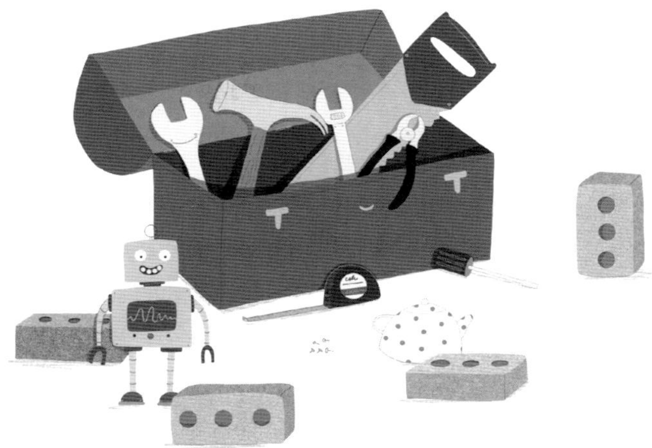

4. **Avoid questions.** Don't dodge the bricks.
5. **Don't break the bricks.** Every idea stays.
6. **Stay in the moment.** It's happening now.
7. **Be specific.** Narrow bricks are stronger bricks.
8. **Toys—they're not necessarily your friends.** Don't get distracted by what they should be.
9. **Don't plan ahead!** Improvise!
10. **Go big!** The bigger the more memorable and the more fun.

Your toolbox is nearly full. Follow these guidelines and your playtime is going to radically change. And by this point, no matter where you are in the book, hopefully you're continuing to intensely play with your kids for ten minutes every day. This book is your guide, but those ten minutes are the real work—and also the real fun.

Now that you've learned to play with training wheels, we're going to teach you to fly. The fun has only just begun.

GUIDES

So before reading the book, I thought "Oh, I know improv! I was a theatre major. I do it all the time with my son." But I was surprised at how the method Chris outlined opened up the play even more. We often will *yes* our son's play: "Oh, we are building a combine harvester? Okay, let's go!" But as I read the book, I realized I very rarely *and*. I tend to let my son dictate the rules of play. But as soon as I added *and*, our adventures became even more dynamic. We were Alice and the Cheshire Cat, and we became pirates looking for treasure sailing the open seas. The Cheshire Cat was the captain and I was a matey, and we sailed to an island and were attacked by a sea monster, but then we asked him if he wanted to be our friend, and we had tea. With each brick he added, I added another one until we were zooming around the room in pirate clothes and wands and crowns. Instead of being passive, I got to help build the world and not only make it more complex, but make it more exciting for me to pretend. This method lets you create something with your kid together, and the look in my son's eyes as we were doing it let me know how important that was.

—Megan Reichelt, librarian and mother of one, from Maryland

Megan was already great at playing with her son, but once she tried these techniques, playtime suddenly got even better. She also exceled at knowing when to add, and when to *guide*.

Everything we've done up until now is rooted in the skills of improvisation. Improv is the key to radically transforming playtime and relationships between adults and kids. However, in improv all players are created equally. While I'm encouraging you to see through the eyes of a child and to engage with kids in a way that is new and might seem childish, you are not a child. The Making It Up Method is not a truly equal relationship.

You are, instead, a *guide*.

And you *can* do this. The more you play this way, the easier it becomes. Don't just think about it, or half-heartedly fake it, or suppose you'll try eventually. Do it. Play intensely. As one of the great fictional guides is famous for saying: "Do or do not, there is no try."

. . . . .

Jenny is six-year-old Caleb's mother. She's an at-home mom, a.k.a. employed in the hardest career on Earth, yet without an actual paycheck. Caleb is her only child, and while she loves him more than anything, she feels like she's not the mother she thought she would be. Between cooking, cleaning, shopping, driving him to swim lessons and playdates, and far more, she's just burned out. There were years of pure joy, but now . . . she's just so tired. She spends most of her free time worried about finding extra odd jobs since her spouse didn't get the raise they'd hoped for. Things are tough.

Jenny picks up a copy of this book, hoping to reconnect with Caleb in a deeper and more meaningful way. She is excited to try the Making It Up Method with him. Saying *yes, and* took some getting used to, but she dives in. She loves the revived feeling of connection. It happens almost right away. In fact, the first improv-based playtime is one of the best times she and Caleb had in years. Still, she notices something. Often, when she engages in the Making It Up Method, she follows the rules, but Caleb doesn't.

Now, Caleb hops off the bus from school, a big smile on his face. On school days, the first ten minutes home have become their time. Jenny didn't plan to designate a specific time to Making It Up, but it sort of happened. Seeing Caleb's excitement for it only deepens Jenny's commitment to try harder to make improv-based play a daily priority.

As they walk into the kitchen, Caleb instantly dives into play mode. He spreads his arms wide and walks in slow motion like an astronaut on the moon. "Captain, I see no sign of life on the planet."

Jenny jumps right in. She's a Trekkie and loves imagining herself on a mission. "Agreed, Spaceman Bob, I—"

"No, I'm not Bob."

"I keep mixing you up with your twin brother. I'm sorry, Spaceman Joe. Look in—"

"My name's Cookie-Ookie."

Jenny's been moving her body like she is doing a spacewalk. Now she makes choking noises. "Something in the atmosphere made me forget you Cookie-Oookie. Oh, I think it's paralyzing my arm now. If only—"

"No, there's an ice cream man coming."

"Wonderful! Ice cream is the only cure . . . "

All right, let's step away from the scene a moment and talk about what's happening. Jenny's doing a fantastic job. She's following the guidelines of Making It Up well. She's moving her body (going big), exploring the environment around them (in the now). She's said yes to every one of Caleb's bricks (accepting the space environment, she's the captain, and so on) and continues to add her own (just keep adding). She hasn't asked a single question (avoid questions) and she definitely didn't plan this either (don't plan).

Yet, despite her great efforts, Caleb's not following along. In fact, in the scene above, he's broken his own bricks, broken Jenny's bricks, and is, in general, not moving the scene forward.

Earlier, I suggested watching the *Bluey* episode "Work" from season 1. If

you haven't yet, go find that episode. You'll see an almost identical situation. Dad and Bluey are playing, but at the beginning, Bluey keeps smashing down Dad's bricks, and rejecting his ideas.

Things like this do happen. Kids can be stubborn. My own kids are certainly no exception. So, what do you do when you're trying to follow these guidelines, but the kids are breaking every rule?

The answer is pretty simple. You keep going, and you keep following the rules.

In the episode, did you notice that Bandit smiled and kept moving forward? In fact, when Bluey told him that he wasn't allowed to be a dancer, he brought the idea back later in the episode. Even though the brick had been denied, he kept it in mind. That's true mastery.

In the scene above, Jenny's bricks were bashed right and left. Yet every time, she cleverly added a new reason to just keep moving forward. If we resume the scene, we might find Caleb starting to join in more. At some point, the kids *will* join in.

The more you follow the rules, and the more you throw yourself into the play, the more the children will learn and copy you.

In psychological practice, there's a particular technique called Parent-Child Interaction Therapy, or PCIT. This technique is used to treat a number of behavior issues and disorders. The first stage of PCIT is centered around the idea that modeling play-based behaviors will draw your kids in. When doing PCIT with my daughter, if she didn't want to engage or connect, I would simply sit there on the floor playing with toys and describing what I was doing. I was astounded during these early sessions to watch her completely pivot from Princess Stubbornhead to a girl completely eager to join in. I hadn't forced her to follow the rules, I hadn't even told her what the rules were. I just kept doing my part.

The same principle holds true in the Making It Up Method.

Ultimately you aren't a partner, you're a guide.

The more you follow the rules, and the more you throw yourself into the play, the more the children will learn and copy you.

When I was a teacher, I'd often partner with my students in improvisation scenes as they were learning. These teens were beginners at improv. In many ways they found it harder than younger children, thanks to peer pressure

If you keep adding bricks and saying yes, pretty soon the kids are going to add bricks and say yes too.

and culture (I'll get more into older kids in Chapter Twelve). While acting one-on-one with these new improv scenes, a *lot* of rules were broken.

I'll admit, there's an impulse to correct someone when they do something wrong. There's part of me that was tempted to say things like, "No, Shayla, you just broke my brick," or "Alisson, you clearly planned that." Yet a funny thing happened the more I taught these skills. I noticed that the *less* I corrected my students, especially in the moment, the more they started to understand the rules on their own. This was especially true when I paired older kids who knew what they were doing with younger students who were new to it.

This will happen in your playtime too. If you keep going, and keep having fun, the kids are going to start having fun too. And if you keep adding bricks and saying yes, pretty soon the kids are going to add bricks and say yes too.

Secret Tip: Kids are natural improv artists. Younger kids are used to playing. They're using bricks all the time. They're building ideas on top of each other from the very beginning. And they learn very quickly the power of *yes, and*. If a playtime is going poorly for whatever reason, don't force it. Just try

doubly hard the next time. We all have our rough days. And I guarantee that if you're doing this daily in ten-minute bursts, the majority of those sessions will be transformative and fun.

Teacher as guide is nothing new.

When I taught theatre, one of my favorite weeks with my Drama One kids involved a "Teacher in Role" scenario that my kids spent a week with. Teacher in Role and Mantle of the Expert are fancy terms we use for times when the teacher plays right alongside the kids in an extended improv. In fact, this particular lesson took a week. During those classes, I was part of the scene as a character who needed to interact with others. Specifically, my kids were exploring medieval theatre in Europe, and I was a monk.

It's fun being part of a scene. You never know quite what's going to happen (don't plan ahead) and you're constantly building off your students' ideas (keep adding,) but in a literal sense, I was never quite the equal of those students. I'm still the teacher, and I still have to guide them.

It's similar in the playtimes with your kids.

Obviously, if everything falls apart one day, let it go. Try again tomorrow. Never scold a kid or try to correct them because they aren't following the rules of improv. I'm in no way advocating enforcement of improv rules. And, crazy enough, I don't want you to teach those rules to the kids either—at least not aloud.

Trust me.

You know the rules. And the more *you* follow them, as the expert, the more those sponge-like kids will absorb. You'll be astounded at how fast they add bricks of their own, or start avoiding questions.

- Don't force.
- Don't correct.
- Just guide.

This work can have long-lasting impacts on your family and on your children, including their confidence and creativity.

And one more important note in this chapter. This is work, yes. I'm redefining your relationships with your kids. This might be some of the most important work you do. It can have long-lasting impacts on your family and on your children, including their confidence and creativity.

Yet, while there's work to it, the process needs to be fun. If you're not having fun because you're stressed about the rules in the last chapter, just relax. Try not thinking about the rules for a few sessions and come back to them when you're ready. The rules will help. However, at its core, each session of Making It Up should be fun for both you and the kids. That's very important.

Transitions

If you're having any trouble, it's likely over transitions. These are tough for anything, but transitions into and out of improv-based play can be particularly tricky.

Depending on your kid, it's worth noting that ten minutes a day every day might take twenty minutes or more of your time. Add a sibling in, and chaos can ensue. I'll get to cheats in a moment, but let's just acknowledge that not everyone can jump in and out of intense play in a heartbeat. If you're new to it, it might be worth adding a few concrete transition moments both to the beginning and the end. Here are four tips that might help:

1. **Routine:** If possible, make the intense playtime occur at the same time in the day each day. Maybe it's right after breakfast or after the kids get home from school. For many kids, knowing *when* in the general day to expect the intense playtime gives both a routine and a moment to look forward to. If possible, try to schedule intense playtime right before or after some easy and daily part of your preexisting schedule.
2. **Transition effect:** Some kids need extra help knowing that something's changing. Try using a handclap or a small bell or a flick on and off of the lights. Some type of sound or signal at the beginning and the end of playtime can show kids when playtime's begun and when it's over. This is similar to a curtain rising and lowering onstage.
3. **Timers:** If you're pressed to carve out those ten minutes and are afraid of your kid going overtime, feel free to set a timer. This gives a nice auditory transition (see above) and a clear boundary for when you're done. This won't be necessary for everyone, but it might help some.
4. **Keep it light:** There's a good chance that some of these play sessions are going to be so great that the kids won't want them to end.

Stopping and transitioning out of intense improv-based play can start to become tricky or hit on behavior concerns. If that occurs, try to stay goofy or positive. Phrases like "I can't wait for tomorrow's play" work, and so might distractions, such as involving them in different activities quickly.

Remember, the more you use the Making It Up Method, the easier these transitions will become.

Cheats

Any teacher or guide knows there are always a few "cheats" to help make things easier. I've mentioned already that there are resources at the back, and at www.ChristopherMannino.com/MIU towards helping think of improv ideas and bricks.

Here are a few other special cheats that might make it easier to guide playtime:

1. **Be Old:** Kids have more energy than us. It's a simple fact. So how are you supposed to constantly keep up with them? One trick is to be old in the playtime. The older the better. Be an ancient, geriatric person who needs to sit. Kids are happy to let "old" characters sit and move less. Feel free to add old voices or mannerisms, and really ham it up. I've had many playtimes where I've managed to sit when I'm exhausted because I'm just "too old" to be running.
2. **Add to Ignore:** I mentioned ignoring the behaviors that aren't in line with improv-based play. There are definitely going to be moments when you simply have to ignore something. While it's tricky to just pretend you didn't hear or see something, adding an instant new brick is an easy way to reinforce the type of play you want while also ignoring the behavior or rule-breaking you don't want to highlight. Adding to Ignore is a great skill you can use a guide.
3. **Be the Kid:** If playtime seems forced at any point, one of the easiest and most successful cheats is to simply reverse roles with your kid. They're the parent, you're the child. This is a guaranteed winner, and you'll be surprised at how eagerly they try to teach you things. If you haven't yet tried this role, it's a definite winning strategy to consider.

4. **Walk Away:** Look, if things are going rough and you just can't make this particular playtime work, it's okay to walk away. Same's true with rough behaviors. This isn't a behavior-focused book, but we all have those rough moments. Don't let one bad playtime spoil it for the next time. If necessary, just walk away. For example, if a kid starts hitting or screaming and gets stuck in their behavior. You can't say "yes" to a hit. It's okay to walk away and try again later.

You're the guide. Not an equal. Yet you're also having fun, and bonding with your kid in ways you've never before experienced. You've some extra tools and tricks at the ready. Next, we'll dive deeper into one of the more challenging aspects of this relationship building.

SPONGES AND ANCHORS

My three-year-old son Senny (short for Seneca) and I have a fun-loving relationship full of imaginative play. Like any relationship, however, it has moments of tension. The *Making It Up* Method helped us round the corner on one of those moments when I expressed my disappointment at yet another potty-training regression involving a heavily soiled *Bluey* pull-up diaper. After changing his diaper and having him sit on the potty to keep the association, Senny's feelings were still unsettled as I brought him up to the changing table to put on another pull-up.

Discussing our different snack options, Senny joked that he wanted to eat me. I typically deflect my three-year-old son's recurring desire to eat me by exclaiming, "I'm not a yumblat (what Martian Mickey Mouse calls hot dogs)," which gets a laugh and lets us move on, but this time I leaned into the *yes, and* system by accepting that I would, in fact, be eaten.

"Oh yeah? What part are you going to eat first?"

I could see the excitement on his face as he realized the game was on.

"Your . . ." he stretched the word, scanning my body with his eyes, "HANDS!"

"Bah! Help!" I immediately yelped, rolling my hands under my arms and poking his belly with my wrists. "I can't change this diaper, I've lost my hands!"

Senny squealed with laughter, then after a minute or so of being prodded by my wrists, spit my hands back out. "Just teasing!"

I resumed pulling on his pants over the diaper only to be interrupted, "Now I ate your nose!"

"Oh no!" I groaned with an overly-nasal voice, "I really need to sneeze! Ahh ahh . . . ahh ahh . . . Help! Help! I can't sneeze!"

Mercifully, Senny spit back out my nose after three or four attempts with his rolling giggle accompanying my "CHOO!"

On and on we went with variations that showed a far more impressive anatomy knowledge base than our typical round of head, shoulder, knees, and toes.

"Now I ate your ears!"

"What?!"

"Your eyes!"

"Who said that? I can't see!"

"Your neck!"

I shrugged my shoulders so my chin lay on my chest, then responded with a hoarse voice, "Help, I can't turn my head! Is someone behind me?"

Finally, thinking he had a checkmate in his pocket, Senny slyly smiled and said through his giggles, "Your mouth!"

Pressing my lips firmly together, I responded with mumbled desperation, "mmm hmm mmm a hmm hmm!" producing one of those rare moments of prolonged belly laughter and leaving the tough parenting moment of impatience, disappointment, and the hurt feelings that go with it at the bottom of the trash can alongside the soiled diaper.

—Chris Gaffney, stay at-home dad and father of two, from Connecticut

Chris was feeling frustrated. He had a moment that could've turned sour. Instead, he focused on the playtime and moved forward. There's a skill to this that involves what I call the *anchor technique*, and it's going to change the way you think about playtime entirely.

I had my own period of frustration two years ago. I stood outside Gavin's school on an early morning in November. This was normally one of my favorite times of day. Instead of dropping him off like the other first grade parents, I'd grown accustomed to parking at the nearby library and walking him up to school so we could talk and spend a few minutes together before he started his day. While he was only six, I knew my years of being the cool dad he actually wanted to hang out with were numbered.

Yet as we walked, I frowned. Something was definitely wrong. His shoulders slumped and he was unusually quiet.

"Something bothering you?" I prompted.

He offered a noncommittal grunt.

"You can always talk to me," I said.

Another grunt. Was he closer to those grumpy teenage years than I'd realized? Was this the end of our morning walks? To be honest, his behavior had been shifting for weeks—moodiness, silent pickups. I'd contacted his teachers, worried he might be getting bullied, but no one could figure out what had caused this shift.

Then he said something that took me a moment to process.

"It's my zoo. I'm worried no one will come. I'll build a great zoo, and I'll work really hard, but what if no matter what's there, I can't get any visitors?"

I'll pause to explain that since he was three, Gavin's loved animals. He's talked many, many times about opening a conservation-focused zoo or animal sanctuary when he's older. Yet that wasn't the concerning part of the sentence I'd heard. The problem was that I'd heard it before, or a very slight variation, from my wife.

You see my wife had opened her own online store just a few months prior. And as any entrepreneur knows, there are moments, especially early on, that are *hard*. One day, she'd expressed her frustration that she had a great site but was worried no one would come.

Kids are built to absorb. It's how they learn.

Now, a month later, that same sentiment was eating at my son, tied to his what-do-you-want-to-do-when-you-grow-up dreams and fantasies.

There's a reason this was happening.

It's important to know, because it's going to affect your playtimes too. Let's start with a rhetorical question. Who lives in a pineapple under the sea? *Your kid*. Okay, maybe kids aren't underwater cartoons, but just like SpongeBob, kids are sponges. Kids are built to absorb. It's how they learn.

Gavin soaked in my wife's frustrations and anxiety. He absorbed the fear—and the very sentence she'd used. Then, over the course of several weeks, that emotion gnawed through him transforming his thoughts and behaviors.

Kids are *Sponges.*

This isn't all bad, of course. The entire last chapter focused on your role as guide. While you guide the play, the kids absorb it. They'll learn just by seeing

you follow the rules. They imitate your behavior and mirror the intense playtime right back at you. You add a brick; they add a brick. You say yes; they say yes. You avoid questions; they avoid questions.

Sponges, indeed! Naturally absorbing every bit of information you give them, whether intentional or not, and learning from every stimuli.

Yes, this ties into the same concern many parents rightly have about what their kids see on TV. They see it, they hear it, they absorb it. A sponge will absorb every bit of water nearby. And sponges are *changed* by the water as well. That hard, stiff sponge becomes soft and malleable. Its entire existence is altered by what it absorbs—just like Gavin was altered by his parents' stress.

It's super important to realize that you cannot control what information they absorb. They simply absorb *everything*. For improv-based play, this is essential to remember.

PAY ATTENTION TO WHAT YOU CARRY INTO PLAYTIME.

Imagine you had an awful day at work. Your boss yelled at you, and you feel so angry that you want to scream. You can't concentrate on anything, much less play with your kids, but you're going to try some Making It Up playtime because you're committed to those ten minutes a day.

Well, how do you think playtime's going to go? Maybe it will be amazing and just what you need. Or maybe it will be horrible, and that anger and frustration will spill out into the nearest sponge: your kid.

Take a moment before playtime to assess your own mental state. Are you calm, collected, and excited? Because whatever baggage you bring into the session is what you're asking your children to shoulder.

NO ONE WANTS THEIR KID TO BE SAD, ANGRY, OR UPSET.

So why feed that into the sponge?

It's not all bad.

The flip side to the sponge metaphor is that kids will absorb anything good you throw at them too. Paying attention to what you carry into playtime can result in either a negative or a positive result. In fact, the entire previous chapter focused on your role as a guide. Beyond modeling good improv, the simplest things you bring into playtime matter the most.

Be sure to pack these four things for every playtime:

1. **Love:** Yes, love. It's the single biggest thing a kid needs. And whether they're your own kid, or a student, or a friend's kid you're babysitting, you can still approach every playtime from a place of love. The kids will absorb that love.
2. **Respect:** You might not be their equal, and sometimes kids can be annoying. Yet we still approach every interaction filled with a deep respect for them and their journey. Saying yes to every brick is an innate way to show respect.
3. **Kindness:** You can't keep adding to a scene, or building up a relationship, if that relationship isn't built on kindness. Building together is a fundamentally kind activity, and part of why this method works so well.
4. **Energy:** Yeah, you're tired. I am too. Doesn't matter. The more energy you can bring into this process, the more energy the kids will mirror—and the quicker the relationship will deepen. If possible, fill that energy up with joy, the strongest energy there is.

It might seem silly to point out love, respect, kindness, and energy, but together they make a big difference. Don't forget that the more joy and respect you bring into your improv-based playtime, the more joy and respect the kids will mirror.

In fact, this is part of why I focused so hard on not directly teaching rules to the kids when you are guiding them through improv. The kids are learning the rules. They're also learning a lot more. They're learning about love, respect, kindness, energy, and patience too. They're seeing that you prioritize them, and that you know how to regulate your emotions when you have stressors.

Anchors

Hold on a moment . . . am I asking you to be happy all the time? Am I saying, lie to the kids? Hide any negative emotions?

No, not exactly.

I have a technique that I've been using for years, which is less about playtime and more about helping you, as an adult, regulate. In fact, this technique has become the foundation for much of my week-to-week success. It's what I call the use of *anchors*.

The stress is real, the fears are valid, but with a little work, they're manageable.

And the more you use anchors, the more you'll realize that they can be a massive support even beyond intense playtime. This is life-changing stuff. So strap in.

For the next section, I want you to set a timer. An actual one on your phone, smart device, sundial, or whatever you use. You're going to set a timer for three minutes and no more. Trust me.

DON'T START YET.

When that timer begins, I want you to think about the bad stuff.

Whatever it is that bothers you. News, politics, climate change, work, relationships, health, etc.

While the timer goes, you're going to close your eyes and let your mind dwell on *all* of it. This is sanctioned internal doomscrolling. But the second that timer stops, I want you to open your eyes and come back to the page. (If you're listening to the audiobook, we're going to record three minutes of silence just for you.)

Alright, are you ready?

Start the timer.

Welcome back. You alright? Yes that sucked big time. You probably feel awful now, and I'm sorry. But there's a method to this madness, I assure you. I want you to think about what just happened. About how it felt. And about the lingering feelings now.

Those three minutes were an example of what I call the *storm*.

The storm is real.

I am not, for a moment, saying those fears aren't valid. And believe me, I have them too. I've got so many doomscroll-style triggers, it's not even funny. I grew up in the shadow of the Cold War, saw the Twin Towers collapse, and survived a global pandemic. When I was a teacher, we had gun incidents on campus. And that's not even touching the little things that are equally troubling, like will it rain tomorrow, and did I remember to turn off the oven or lock the door? And what about that job you interviewed for, or that first date coming up, or that election you don't want to miss . . . and so on.

The storm *is* real.

If you'll take this metaphor a step further and envision yourself as a ship moving forward toward great intense playtimes, the *only* way you're going to weather storms like this is with an anchor. The first step toward creating an anchor is to acknowledge one of the fundamental causes of these storms: *time travel.*

No, that's not a misprint. I might be training you to fight dragons long-term, but there's absolutely nothing speculative about this type of time travel. In fact, you just time traveled for three minutes, using a timer.

Think about it. During those three minutes, where were you? Were you safe, in your house or wherever you chose to read? On an external level, you never left that comfort and safety.

Yet *internally,* we stray. Again, I'm no stranger to this.

Yoda from the film *Star Wars: The Empire Strikes Back* famously says: "Never your mind on where you are, what you are doing!" It's poignant because for many of us, it's true. We live in a time traveler's paradise. From TikTok to YouTube, newsfeeds to meme dumps, we're constantly diverting our attention.

THE STORM IS A FORM OF TIME TRAVEL.

You're worried about something coming up. A meeting, a deadline, a party, a returned email. Or you're worried about something behind you. An opportunity that didn't go as planned, a response you hadn't expected, some news you can't shake. Even if what's upsetting you is the most current of current events, chances are you're still mentally travelling to get to the storm.

Why? Because we're conditioned to seek it out. For many people, the storm is all we know. We travel from stress to stress, worry to worry. Believe me, I used to be one of those people.

When the storm arrives, you need to drop an anchor.

And here's the kicker: **if you bring the storm into playtime, you'll hurt your relationships with the kids**. It might not happen at once, but the more baggage you carry, the more they'll absorb, and the greater that stress will build within them. I'll never forget when Gavin looked at me with those wide eyes, worried no one would come to his imaginary zoo. I knew we'd carried the storm to him.

The remedy to this time-traveling, doomscrolling, storm-searching baggage is the anchor.

I'll admit I'm a fan of the time travel British TV show *Doctor Who*. And as any *Doctor Who* fan will tell you: the answer to time travel problems is always *more* time travel! Well, in this case it works. When the storm arrives, you need to drop an anchor.

An anchor is a memory. It is an intense emotional moment that you experienced, preferably in the not-too-distant past. The key to a good anchor is that it has to be a memory that evoked an overwhelmingly strong positive emotion in you personally.

Because everyone's anchors are unique, no two people will share the same anchors. The anchor has to have a deep, personal connection to you. We'll gather some potential anchors in a moment.

Several months ago, I was struggling. I'd just started a new day job and was in over my head. Money was tight at home, and stress was building. And there was the news. I was doomscrolling a lot. Another mass shooting. Climate change growing. The world felt like it was spinning faster and faster, threating to pop right off its axis and tumble into open space like a flung marble.

The storm surrounded me.

It hung like a proverbial raincloud over my head wherever I walked, drenching me in gloom and spilling stress onto all those around. And when rain's spilling, the sponges soak it in. Gabby and Gavin grew grumpy. They fought and bickered and yelled, until I realized that I'd brought the storm to them.

I needed an anchor.

A week earlier, I'd spent a day as a substitute teacher at Gabby's preschool. I'd been asked to cover preschool gym. Of all my substitute teaching experiences, it was one of the best days I've ever had. Gym to five-year-olds isn't particularly difficult (we had a mock snowball fight). But the real joy was seeing Gabby in her school environment. She beamed and showed me such joy—marching into that class, pointing to me, and saying loudly, "Look everyone, that's my daddy. He's the gym teacher. Gym Teacher Daddy. That's him. Right there."

The night of that substitute day, I put Gabby to bed. At the end of her routine, after the teeth were brushed, the stories were read, and a kiss had been left upon her forehead, she asked me to pause.

"Daddy, wait."

"What is it?"

"Daddy . . . you're the best daddy ever. I loved you as my teacher. I love you so much, Daddy." She smiled then, and I swear the entire room lit up like a lamp with the glow of that expression. My heart melted right out of my chest, forming a puddle on the floor as I gave her another kiss good night.

Boom.

Anchor found.

That moment of joy became my newest anchor.

The anchor was not the day substitute teaching, though it was wonderful. It wasn't the bedtime routine, or the story, or the kiss beforehand. The specific moment of that heartfelt praise and that huge glowing smile—that was the moment. Specifically, it was the emotion *I* felt that made it such a strong anchor.

This was a moment of intense pride, love, and joy. A moment in time when there was no storm, no clouds, no fears at all.

I had my newest anchor.

So, back to the stress-filled week I'd mentioned. I knew what I needed to do. I dropped my anchor and clung to it.

EVERY TIME A STORM RISES, FOCUS ON YOUR ANCHOR.

I'm not exaggerating when I say this changes everything. It doesn't matter if the glass is half full or half empty, because if you're worried about the glass, look somewhere else!

No, the stressors won't vanish. But your attention doesn't need to dwell on them. Because really, are you helping anyone by dwelling in the storm?

In this vein, it can be truly helpful to use an anchor before playtime. What does that mean? Right before you're supposed to be engaging in intense improv-based play, focus on a deeply positive emotional memory. Remember that sponge-like kids will absorb what you bring into playtime. If you're bringing *intense joy* into the playtime, they'll absorb that!

And it's worth noting that an anchor doesn't have to be an overall positive experience. It simply has to create a profoundly positive emotion in you. If possible, it should have a visual memory associated with it: the stronger you can visualize that anchor, the easier it becomes to use.

One of the strongest anchors I carried for some months occurred when I first took the kids to Universal Studios in Florida. We'd been given a free pass for the day during a longer trip to Disney, and bluntly, the kids were too young for Universal. We were walking through the Diagon Alley section of Harry Potter World. I stood with my wife and parents, when Gavin, then five, ran just ahead of us, filled with excitement and energy.

There is a life-size dragon feature above the Gringotts Bank. I was admiring it when an actual fireball burst from its mouth in a feat of impressive pyrotechnics. Gavin pivoted, stricken with terror. He ran to me, grabbed my leg, and was sobbing that he wanted to leave.

This moment became an anchor.

Why? On its face, it was a rather sad moment, with my son literally shaking in fear. Still, this was a strong anchor because *my* emotions at the time were intense and positive. Gavin ran straight to me and *needed* me in that moment. I was his source of strength, safety, and comfort. Even in the moment, I felt a deep sense of love, pride, and gratitude that I meant so much to him. And the visual memory of my son fleeing a fireball was pretty unique.

I had my anchor.

And I used it.

In the weeks that followed, whenever I felt a storm rising, I turned to that anchor. Whenever I felt annoyed at some behaviors, such as the kids fighting, I recalled the anchor. And that anchor remained until I replaced it with a new one.

I NEVER TRAVEL WITHOUT AN ANCHOR.

I bring my anchor everywhere—not just to playtime, but everywhere I go. There's also a reason I advocate for a specific, strong memory as opposed to a distraction. Yes, distractions help. Instead of the news, maybe think about the book you're reading, or the movie coming out next week, or that song you love. Those are great. But they aren't anchors. Ultimately, an anchor is what moors you back to what matters: those hugs from your kids, that special smile from your spouse, that moment of pride at work. Whatever happened is real and it matters and it's yours. *Use it.*

So, on that note, let's spend a few minutes gathering anchors.

It's important to realize these will change frequently, the fresher the memory, the stronger the anchor. Still, I want you to prepare another three-minute timer, and this time go the opposite direction. Think about a moment you felt amazing. Your personal feeling and connection in that moment are what matter most. Ideally this is something from the past month or two. A moment when you were on top of the world. Think hard, because you want the strongest possible memory.

If you think you've got one, get ready.

When the timer starts, close your eyes and imagine every detail. What did you see, hear, and feel in that moment? What emotional response did it create? Do your best to recall every detail.

When you're ready, start the timer for three minutes.

. . . . .

Welcome back.

At the beginning of the chapter, we had three minutes of storm.

Now, you've experienced three minutes of anchor.

Do you see how different they feel?

Now, you're starting to grasp the anchor's secret: by clutching the anchor, you ignore the storm.

Before you forget the moment you experienced, fill it in below. If you're on audio or eBook, grab a paper or use a note-taking app on your phone. Write down the anchor.

And *remember* this anchor the next time you're not in the mood for playtime. In fact, if you're up to it, I highly suggest trying to think of at least one other possible anchor as a backup.

My anchor is:
When it happened, I felt:
Some key moments I remember (sights, sounds) that will help me recall the anchor:

> **On the surface, it's easy to think that relying on an anchor is a way to sidestep reality, to put the hard parts on the back burner. In practice, when conjuring the anchor moment, the one filled with joy, light, and peace, I'm reminded that that is my reality. The anchor is a reminder that I choose what is important, I make my meaning, and that the difficult, frustrating, impossible moments are as fleeting as the rest.**
>
> **—Lisha Curry, adolescent therapist and mother of one, from Delaware**

Remember, kids are sponges. They'll pick up on what you do and how you do it. Those storms are real, but an anchor can help you weather them and continue to build joy with the kids. There's another related secret that can help too. Perhaps the biggest trick or hack of all. That's coming in the next chapter, when I teach you *magic*.

MAGIC

I've been doing the *yes, and* technique during play with my daughters for years. For all the dads who aspire to reach the gold standard set by Bluey's dad, this is your ladder. It's meaningful core-memory building time with your kids, and exposure therapy for your social anxiety rolled into one!"

—Philip Weseman, stay-at-home dad of two, from Missouri

I've mentioned *Bluey* a few times. And if you've seen the show, chances are you want to parent like Bandit and Chili, Bluey's parents. However, there's one criticism of the show that's hurled around far more than any other: How do the parents have the *energy* for all that playing? It's a valid question. Sometimes those cartoon characters are just too animated.

Yes, the pun was wonderful, but the question remains.

This type of intense improv is tiring. It can take a lot of energy. Kids have unlimited reserves of energy. I keep hearing about clean energy or the potential of nuclear fusion when the real energy source is in front of our eyes: hamster wheels large enough for the kids to run in. Wheels that power generators somehow. Throw the kiddos in there whenever they're cooped up and boom—world energy crisis solved. Okay, I jest, but some kids are seriously tireless.

On top of that, parenting is exhausting.

I love my kids, and I love being a parent. For over seven years my sole job was a stay-at-home dad. And it was the greatest job I ever had. It was also the hardest work and the lowest paying.

Children can be exhausting from day one. You've likely been building excitement and anticipation for months, but nothing fully prepares you for the weariness of parenting. Especially if your kids aren't good sleepers. Yeah, mine are not. My wife and I joke that there must have been a moment in

the hospital, right before delivery, when doctors slipped a bunch of forms in front of us. Somewhere on those forms there was a "sleeping model: yes/no" question, and we were too tired to check the correct box. Now, I hear so many lovely stories of kids who sleep through the night . . .

Not mine.

Which brings me back to square one.

The kids are ready for playtime. They're so energized that they're bouncing off the walls. And you . . . well, you've just fallen out of bed, searching for a few gallons of coffee. Your body doesn't move the way it should, and everything hurts. Oh, what's that? You want me to *play* now?

Can'tIjustgobacktosleepI'msotiredI'llbeupsoonIswearzzzzzzzzzzzz

. . . . .

There is a secret to finding the energy to play with kids. And no, it's not coffee, though I am a big coffee fan.

THE SECRET IS THEATRE.

Yep, more theatre. And remember, that doesn't mean this book is for theatre people, it just means I'm teaching everyday people how to use theatre techniques to transform your play.

Now before I tell you this secret, recall that the improv skills in theatre have already changed everything. If you're following those guides, I'll bet you've had some of the most intense playtimes ever, and the playtimes will only continue to deepen and strengthen the bond between you and the kids.

The more you use these skills the better you and the kids become, and those bricks go higher and higher.

After the improv skills, I took a break to discuss the power of anchors. In the last chapter, I focused on anchors as an essential tool to help focus on positivity when there's a lot of other stuff around. I strongly encourage anchor use. It's a life-changer. And here's the surprise . . . while the terms are mine, the skills are rooted in more theatre skills. The anchor technique is an adaptation of a form of method acting that employs an *emotional recall.* This skill allows actors to draw on a very specific emotion they've experienced when playing a character. And trust me, there are times onstage when there are a million other things on your mind. Those anchors are essential for those performances, and that skill can transform your daily routine as well.

In other words, if you've made it this far, you're already a theatre pro! And you didn't even have to audition.

[The camera pans out to reveal a luxuriously-dressed crowd rising to their feet in applause, for YOU, the reader, and the amazing work you are doing so far.]

Alright, with that in mind, back to energy. Yeah, this isn't as hard of a chapter or as big of a secret, but it honestly works. At the root of all theatre is the same essential skill: *faking it.*

Fake It

Acting is fake.

I'm not saying this as an insult. It's the nature of the art.

The actors on stage and screen are not the characters they're playing. The lines are written for them. The sets are fake. The costumes are fake. And the emotions . . . yes, they're drawn from truths (see last chapter) but are ultimately fake too.

AND THAT'S THE SECRET TO ENERGY IN PLAYTIME.

Fake it.

That's it.

Now, I can guess what you're thinking. It's likely along the lines of: "Well, Chris, up to now, every chapter of the book's been filled with super-useful and mind-blowing stuff. I'm enjoying it. But . . . now we're to the part on energy. I mean, I really need help with this. I'm always way too tired to play with the kids. I just don't have the kind of energy they do. And your million-dollar solution is just fake it?"

When you *act* energetic, it creates energy.

Yep. That's it.

When you *act* energetic, it creates energy. Any actor can tell you this. And this is backed by research as well. In 2021, researchers at Penn State published a study that smiling reduced stress and increased happiness. The key finding emphasizes that even faked and forced smiles produced the same results.[1] In a similar study published by the *Southern Economic Journal* in 2020, smiling, including forced and fake smiles, was found to definitively improve social communications.[2] What's going on in these studies? Faking a smile creates happiness?

Yes.

Go on, try it. Give a smile right now, even a fake one. I bet it helps your mood. In a similar vein, the *act* of pretending to be energetic can create energy. However, this comes with a caveat. Smiling is a simple physical act. Faking energy might take a bit more, especially if the kids are wired. So let's turn to some of those theatre skills for help. I'll break it into nice easy steps, and between any step, feel free to take a sip of coffee.

STEP ONE: START WITH VOICE

When the body is weary, it can be hard to run or jump or do whatever else the kids are demanding. The easiest thing to fake is the voice. Using a big voice requires extra breath, which in turn gets your heart pumping and your lungs full. This is the beginning of extra energy.

STEP TWO: ONE ARM AT A TIME

Just as we lift one leg at a time to walk, lifting a single arm is a great second step toward faking energy. If you're too tired to stand, wave with your arm and do it bigger and bigger. Each movement carries a little bit more energy with it.

STEP THREE: FINGERS, FINGERS, FINGERS

Okay, the arm's moving, now feel the energy in your fingers. Fingers are one of the most integral parts of communication and if you start tensing and

untensing them, you're going to feel that energy spread everywhere. Point to the sky, to the kid, to yourself. Feel it.

STEP FOUR: BE A MIRROR

Even with your growing energy, sometimes we can't think of how to move or what to do. If that's the case, mimic the kids. They're up, try being up. They're down, be down. When you're really tired, sometimes just thinking about the required motion is taxing, so let them do the thinking.

STEP FIVE: TUG THE ANCHOR

Feeling a bit stressed? Tiredness goes hand in hand with the storm. It's easy to give in to negativity at this point, so hold your anchor close. The anchor itself is ideally filled with positive energy. Siphon some of that from your mind into your body. And remember, playtime is only ten minutes. You can do this.

STEP SIX: KEEP GROWING

You don't have to go from zero to breakdancing in a heartbeat. A little bit at a time makes a big difference. Every time you swing your arm, swing a bit harder. Every time you point, point with more energy. Let the voice grow, the movements grow, and as you're going, let the energy within you grow as well.

These steps really will help. Remember, at the end of the day and the end of the play, faking energy is okay. The more energy you fake, the more you'll create. And the more you create, the stronger bonds you'll build.

. . . . .

Let's see what this looks like in action. Imagine Tom, a stay-at-home dad to Julie, a precocious and highly energetic five-year-old.

Julie: I'm going to the moon!

Tom: Yep. [Tom is feeling tired, and a bit stressed about work. He did notice that Julie added a brick, and intense playtime has begun. He knows he should try, for their sake. But he's really sleepy.]

Julie: Fly with me, Daddy! [She extends her arms and runs in circles.]

Tom: Zoom! [While Tom is far too tired to fly in circles, he forces a medium-volume voice. It isn't the biggest effort. He also realizes he hasn't yet added a single brick.] Watch out for that meteor!

Julie: Oh no, I'm hit! [She flails her arms, falling to the ground.]

Tom: An intruder has landed on our planet. [His energy is starting to build. Seeing Julie accept his brick, without much effort from him, was a bit exciting. Now, trying to fake the energy more, he again resorts to a voice, this time a funny one.]

Julie: Oh no, the space robot king. I have to fix my ship.

Tom: [He's still too tired to fully get up, but he moves an arm, swinging it like a giant periscope. He also adds a bit more energy to his robot voice.] Where is the intruder. Activating scanners. Scanning the area.

Julie: [Curls up, hiding her face.] They'll never find me.

Tom: [Covers his own face, mirroring her.] Scans complete, child detected. [He goes to rise but is swept by a wave of exhaustion

> **and some stress. He remembers the job worries that kept him up last night. In response, he quickly tugs on his anchor, a memory of playing outside with Julie and his wife Karen. They fell in the mud but couldn't stop laughing. The anchor helps refocus him. He swings his arm back up, and now stands.] You are the intruder. Now you must pay the price, and dance!**
>
> **Julie: Nooooooo! [She stands and starts to dance.] Your dancing powers are working, but I have a secret weapon . . .**

The above example could go on for however long the playtime needs. Note that throughout the play, Tom was both exhausted and distracted. Yet he still followed the rules of improv and still had a fantastic Making It Up play session. He was able to fake his own energy, which kept the playtime going, and helped build those bonds. By the end of their time together, he felt more energized and happy, a natural consequence of this technique.

Yes, faking it works. After all, the entire method in this book is a fancy way of making it up.

SOME MORE TIPS TO STAY ENERGIZED:

- **Water**—One of the biggest causes of fatigue is dehydration. Try a drink of water before playtime.
- **Music**—Some people respond well to external stimuli. I often play music to energize myself. If you're feeling low-key, try putting on some music in the background. It might even become a brick of its own.
- **Sunshine**—The biggest source of energy in the solar system is that ball of gas hanging out in the sky. Feel free to take the playtime outside, weather permitting. Sunshine can truly invigorate.
- **Anchors**—Is your anchor strong enough? Are you thinking hard about it? An anchor isn't just stabilizing, it's energizing. Consider if yours needs a tweak.
- **Delay**—Don't forget, you determine when the intense playtime occurs. If all else fails and you're really too tired, do it later!

In the next chapter, we're taking everything we've learned on the road. But we've been through a lot so far, so let's recap. I do hope you're seeing the results of your intense playtimes already. Remember, reading the book won't be enough, you have to actually *do* it.

RECAP CHEAT SHEET

1. **Ten minutes a day, no distractions.**
2. **Say *yes, and* to all bricks.**
3. **Keep adding.**
4. **Avoid questions.**
5. **Don't break the bricks.**
6. **Stay in the moment.**
7. **Be specific.**
8. **Toys—they're not necessarily your friends.**
9. **Don't plan ahead!**
10. **Go big!**
11. **Be a guide, not an equal.**
12. **Have a strong anchor at all times.**
13. **Kids are sponges.**
14. **Fake the energy to grow it.**

Got all that? Great . . . let's take it to the next level.

ADVENTURES

Our play session was an adventure for both of us. We used our wands to fly over the mountains and swim under the sea, until I suddenly lost my wand and my daughter needed to save me.

—Neil Drought, stay-at-home dad, bookkeeper, and father of one, from Milton Keynes, UK

I spent seven years as a stay-at-home dad, like Neil. The adventures are wonderful, but it wasn't always that way. When I first left my teaching career, I fell into a pit of isolation. It was a shock, to be sure. As a teacher at a massive high school theatre program, I'd interacted with hundreds of people a day. I had six classes, multiple after-school programs, parents and other staff to coordinate with, and was just constantly on the go. Then, in a flash, my entire world imploded. From hundreds, my new social circle was now *one*.

Don't get me wrong, becoming a SAHD (stay-at-home dad) was the best decision I ever made. I will always be grateful for the time I spent with my kids. Yet, it was jarring. And I was also *the guy*. I didn't know a single other at-home dad at the time. It made sense, of course. As a public school teacher, my salary was half of my wife's, and my entire take-home pay was funneled straight to a daycare we hated. Yes, it made sense for me to stay home, but that didn't stop that sense of implosion.

So, I tried going out. I started, as many do, with playgrounds and library storytimes. And to be completely honest, the sense of isolation really grew. Because I was on those playgrounds with my baby, surrounded by moms. Don't get me wrong, moms are awesome. And I've nothing but respect for SAHMs (stay-at-home moms). But, there's a definite gap at times between the moms and the sole dad. That sense of isolation only deepened further.

I was rescued from this phase by a book called *The Ultimate Stay-at-Home*

Dad by Shannon Carpenter, who would later become a friend. In it, Shannon discussed the idea of the "Dadventure," an outing with the kids taken once a week. These aren't just the trips to the library storytime or to the playground; these are the trips *everywhere*. His idea is that kids don't really care where they go, they just want to spend quality time with their parents. So why limit yourself to the typical kiddie zones? Soon after reading, the Dadventure became an essential part of my week. Trips to parks, museums, cities, and places I'd never been. These trips became my favorite part of my at-home parenting career.

Soon, I realized the Dadventures could be more. Why just look at a museum? Why not play? Or play in the car?

On the very first page of this book, I talked about a time I picked up the kids. Everyone was gloomy and grumpy. So, I pretended to drive through an array of dragons and wild apes. Everyone's mood pivoted 180 degrees. That silly, fun, improv energy isn't limited to the house. It's something I took on adventures, in the car, and everywhere.

So, strap the kids in, because it's time to take improv-based parenting with us on the road. Note, this chapter, more than any other, is geared mostly toward parents. If you're a teacher, you're still going on those field trips. I recall taking a group of high schoolers up to Manhattan for a field trip and trying to keep the improv-based play flowing even on the bus. So read on, and adapt for your situation.

Taking It on the Road

START SMALL

Okay, I fully recognize this chapter is a pivot. Until now, nothing's had an audience. There have been no crowds watching you play with your kids (just the grocery store shoppers).

Yes, there are other people in the world. Yes, some of those people might see you.

Who cares?

The hardest part of intense play out of the home is the feeling of being judged. For many of us, myself included, there is nothing more personal than our parenting style or our relationship to our kids. Now, if you're reading this and you're a caregiver or teacher, bravo—you've done these skills with an audience on a daily basis. For the rest of us, it might get tricky, but I know you can do it.

No one else who might see you matters. All that matters is your strong connection with your kid.

Why?

Because the truth is, no one else who might see you matters. All that matters is your strong connection with your kid.

That said, let's start as small as possible. That means your backyard, if you have one. A playground if you don't. And for this type of interaction, don't worry about a full ten-minute playtime. Treat those as separate for a while. For now, just borrow some of the skills you have learned from the book and bring them outdoors. Say yes to one brick. Or go big, even if it feels silly.

Some people are going to do this easily, but it's okay if this feels out of your comfort zone. Start small, start simple.

If your kid spreads their arms and makes an airplane noise, maybe hold up your hand to your mouth like a microphone and say "Clear for landing."

If your kid sees a dragon behind the slide, help them ready a magic sword.

If the kid tells you it's time to visit China, start digging that tunnel.

Saying yes to a brick *in public* is the first step on the adventures to come.

WEAR BLINDERS

Remember the anchor technique? Hopefully you're carrying those emotional anchors with you everywhere you go. Well, this handy *blinders* technique is quite similar. The idea is simple. When in public, only focus on the kid. The anchor provides a specific, concrete, positive memory to focus attention on so that you can ignore the storm of distractions. In a similar manner, the blinders are emotional barriers put up so that you ignore everyone else.

This is easier than it sounds, for some. To really help zero in on the kid, pick a very specific feature—a specific eye, for example, and place all your attention on that. Yeah, it sounds a little odd only focusing on their eye or their ear. But watch it as it moves; focus on it. The more you zero in on that, the stronger the blinders become, and the easier it is to forget that [*gasp*] there are other people around!

So as your kid zooms around in a spaceship, don't focus on anything except that one eye (even when it's facing away) and use all your energy to direct yourself right into the playtime. You've started small, you're wearing blinders, now join in.

USE THE ENVIRONMENT

Remember back in the rules chapter, when we said toys can be either good or bad? It's true that toys are tricky, in terms of improv. The opposite is true of environment. In theatre we refer to this as the set. And wherever you are, *that* is your set. Your stage, so to speak.

If you're in your backyard, a puddle is an ocean. A sandbox, a desert. A play castle . . . well, that one is whatever you think it is. Doesn't have to be a castle. Could be a robot, a store, or a rocket.

Playgrounds are built for three things. The first is exercise, the second is social play, but the third is imagination. This is why so many playgrounds have abstract features. *Use* those. And as you're playing intensely with the kid, run around the playground. Go down the slide.

No one cares. In fact, I would far rather see adults enjoying time on the playground with their kids than sitting on the side, staring at their phones.

AVOID DISTRACTIONS

This means the phone. Yeah, if you're out and about, your phone is on you. It's the tether each of us carries. I know how tempting it is to pull that screen out. At this point we have evolved (or devolved) to a state where human beings can hardly exist in the wild without our smartphones. It's quite possible that future generations will emerge from the womb, phone in hand, already texting.

That no distractions rule from earlier is even more important now.

PUT THE PHONE AWAY.

Now, there's one other distraction that's also insidious. I've seen this one many times. In fact, we used to notice that at large gatherings of kids in our neighborhood, a similar event occurred each time. The kids would play, and my wife and I would play with them. We'd join in, at their request. Meanwhile, the other adults would clump off and only engage with each other.

Yes, grown-up bonding is fine. But right now, during the intense playtime with your kids, other adults are not the focus. Your kid doesn't want to see you talking football scores or griping about traffic or whatever. You're there for them.

No distractions.

. . . . .

All right, we've got four new tools. We're starting small, wearing blinders, using our environment, and avoiding distractions.

Now it's up to you. Each time you take a risk in public, remember the rewards: the smiles on your kids' faces and the bond you're building. For me, many of the most memorable and meaningful play sessions I've had happened in public. As Shakespeare tells us: "All the world's a stage."

Once you've had a few moments in your backyard or playground, try aiming further afield. These can be places you'd go normally, like a grocery store, or places you might not visit regularly, like a museum. The rules of Making It Up Method play all apply, but each situation will feel a bit different. I'm going to zero in on two likely scenarios, and some tips and tricks.

Scenario One: The Store

Whether it's a grocery store, a department store, or my wife's much-loved outlet clothing store, at some point you're going to be shopping with kids around. If you're lucky, this will take place in the Shangri-La of store types, the absolute pinnacle of human achievement: the bookstore. While there, be sure to recommend a few copies of this book. Okay, maybe I'm a bit biased.

At any rate, stores can be necessary or fun, but to kids, especially young kids, the difference between a store and a playground is minimal. You're in a predefined space with colorful, new things all around, and it's not home. If they're small enough, they're riding in a shopping cart. In other words, a ride at the playground.

Grocery stores come with a built-in obstacle. You need to get shopping done. The example from chapter one where Gabby and I were shopping at Trader Joe's and she had to keep melting me wasn't only real, it was routine. Grocery shopping became a highlight of my week: a time to bond intensely with the kid, while also getting a necessary chore out of the way. In fact, shortly after she started preschool, I would walk into that Trader Joe's and be met with confused stares from the grocery workers.

"Where are the kids? Are you able to shop alone? That sounds . . . boring."

And they're right. Shopping can be boring. But with kids, it can be amazing. It can be a fun bonding time, and it really helps with behavior too. The root issue for misbehavior in younger kids is boredom. Bring them to a boring environment, and you're asking for misbehavior. Engage them in a meaningful way in that environment to completely alter the expectations.

Stores are a great place for typical improv. Let bricks happen. Let a silly voice out, or make your body freeze. If you can tie it into what you need, even better.

"Cowboy, them thar grapes need to be lassoed into this here shopping cart!"

Use bricks and try just saying yes. Saying *yes, and* in public reinforces the skill more strongly than anything you'll do at home. It takes courage to freeze, knowing people are looking at you. This is why when people watch *Bluey* they think the parenting is unattainable—the parents dance in public, or freeze, or pretend to be children. In many of the most memorable episodes, Mum and Dad are out in the real world (including at places like stores) engaged in improv-based parenting.

Try it.

THINGS TO LOOK OUT FOR:

Needs. While shopping, remember that you do need to also shop. Don't forget what you went there for!

Safety. I don't let my kids out of my line of sight in a store, which is something we might do at home. Also be careful to follow the store's rules. Yet at the same time, remember there are real rules, and then there are expectations. No store has a written rule saying no silliness, or no living robots, or no kid-powered freeze rays.

Scenario Two: The Crowd

Okay, so this one covers every situation where there are a lot of kids. We talked about playgrounds, and if the playground is super crowded, this scenario comes into play too. Simply put, the more crowded with kids, the trickier any intense playtime with you is going to be.

In particular, I'm thinking about children's museums. I have three wonderful children's museums within driving distance to me. These are places that can be ideal for intense playtime, as they are designed for playing. At the Please Touch Museum in Philadelphia, for instance, there's a section devoted to a mock grocery store, and a mock bakery/pizza restaurant. This is just one section, but a good example of a place where it's easy to play along with the kids.

In theory.

The trick is that there's often huge crowds. And many, many kids.

The more kids around, the more distracted your kids will be. That's fine. Let them have social playtime with others. Not everything the kid does has to be with you. However, if you do find a quieter area of the museum and can engage in intense improv-style play, do it! My favorite section for this—which

I've seen in every kid's museum I've visited—involves giant foam building blocks. These sections are named various labels: imagination playground, time to build, construction area, etc. But in general, they are all similar: foam cylinders and bricks that can be used to construct anything at all. This is the *perfect* place to try some improv as you are quite literally adding *bricks* to the play, both in terms of ideas and with the foam. Use that environment, say *yes, and,* and keep adding.

Again, the crowd can be a meaningful place for play. The museum, playground, amusement park, or zoo can be places to let that imagination shine.

Or not.

THINGS TO WATCH OUT FOR:

Overstimulation. Crowds have an energy all their own. This isn't about faking energy, like in the last chapter; this is about controlling it. And too much energy or stimulation in playtime isn't going to build, it's going to detract. The key is to know when not to try the intense playtime. If you're in the Magic Kingdom and on a ride, don't try and build a scene. You've spent a small fortune to be there, and you're having fun, and there are tons of crowds and stimuli in every direction. Then again, if you're in a one-hour line with your bored kids at the Magic Kingdom, some improv-based play can be perfect. It teaches kids how to deal with that wait and boredom, and it keeps the day fun.

Safety. Keep those kids close, keep them safe. In crowds, things get crazy. Kids can try to run. If it's not safe for intense playtime, don't even try. Safety first.

. . . . .

TAKE RISKS. SING IN PUBLIC. PLAY ROBOT AT THE GROCERY STORE. GO ON ADVENTURES!

On one day in summer, I dropped Gavin off at a summer day camp. I then drove to Valley Forge, Pennsylvania with Gabby, who was four at the time. Why? Well, I've always liked history, it was beautiful weather, and I wanted to spend some quality, intense playtime with my daughter. Valley Forge is a monument now, essentially a memorial to a winter-long really important peptalk. "What's this place?" she'd asked.

I thought for a moment. "Well, a while back, there was this big match. The Yanks were down at the half, then regrouped, fighting bitter cold, famine, and disease. George Washington provided the best peptalk the world had ever seen, and the Americans went on to score big (with a French assist) and clinch the title (of independence)."

This stellar (and not inaccurate) description earned me only a blank stare.

"Okay, it was the moment that changed things.The rebels had been losing, freezing to death on Hoth, but they went on to defeat the Empire—without even needing to blow up a Death Star."[1]

More blank stares.

The one-man comedy show wasn't going to cut it. And it didn't matter. Valley Forge is a wide-open area, accessible by self-driving tour. And at each stop, you have two options: learn about a really depressing, somewhat inspirational, and potentially pivotal moment in American history. Or, forget about what happened two centuries back, and engage in pure, awesome, intense play.

I chose the latter, and I'm glad I did.

We moonwalked across what had been a fort and held a mock battle near the cannons. We spied fairies dancing near an enormous stone monument. We ate a picnic lunch, dodging ogres.

And yes, other people saw us. I wasn't trying to be disrespectful. I want to go back when the kids are older perhaps. But in the spirit of independence, I allowed the intense bonding between Gabby and I to flourish. This wasn't a battle, or a camp filled with endurance; it was a pure victory.

There's a very real side effect to these adventures. The more you try, the more self-confidence you'll gain. Imagine those bricks building strong bonds with every playtime. Those same bricks are building *you* up. Your confidence and self-esteem will grow, and your own enjoyment will as well.

Unfortunately, not everything in the Making It Up Method is fun and games, as we'll explore next.

BUMPS

I'm a musician, so music plays into a lot of how I interact with the world. Sometimes I'll start singing about what I'm doing, especially if it isn't going right and I'm feeling frustrated. What I've found, to my surprise, is my kids started responding by adding a new lyric of their own to my song, often building on the melody or rhythm or creating a rhyme structure with whatever I had just sung. It has become a way to laugh about moments of misplaced items or messes made.

My kids are a little older, ages twelve and nine, so getting them to actually play pretend these days is a little trickier than it used to be. However, they do often ask amazing and silly "what if" questions about the world. So, I try goading them into giving more details, or I'll add some of my own, essentially a form of *yes, and* that is sometimes countered with no, but by my children. Here's an example:

> Son: A keytar exists. What if you combined a guitar and a saxophone?
>
> Me: Oooo, that's an interesting idea! What would you call it?
>
> Son: A guitarophone? No. A saxotar!
>
> Me: Yes! You would make it make a sound by blowing into it, just like a melodica. Maybe it would blow through the strings somehow. Maybe the strings are made of brass.
>
> Son: No, it's just the strings sound like a saxophone. But they come out of the guitar through a big bell like a saxophone.

We also use moments of, say, misspeaking and mixing up syllables or misunderstanding an idiom to imagine what that would actually look like. One time my daughter heard about two people having a thumb war and ended up drawing an amazing cartoon of two disembodied thumbs with little angry faces and sweat bands on their heads preparing to fight each other in a boxing ring. These kinds of silly moments

have been so helpful, especially on super busy days. My schedule has often kept me from being able to be with them for long stretches after school or in the evenings, so those small memorable moments of connection are crucial.

—Mary Casiello, musician and mother of two, from Massachusetts

Mary sings, even when things aren't going right or she's feeling frustrated. As a musician, her anchor technique is rooted in song. Notice how her kids picked up on her anchor and her energy, absorbing the melody like sponges. This transitioned perfectly into an intense playtime. It works. As she mentions, for busy parents especially, the connections gained in these moments are invaluable. Bumps will happen, but we're going to look at how anchors like Mary's singing can carry us up and over the rough patches.

Luckily for parents everywhere, kids are easy. You placed your order online, and they arrived painlessly, wrapped snugly in that cardboard box from the stork, complete with a detailed instruction manual. Nothing ever goes wrong, and though they need occasional updates, they're just angels from the moment they arrive until the moment you send them off on their own. Every playtime is magnificent. You've incorporated all the rules and guidelines in this book, and both you and the kids are instant experts at improv-based play.

Or not.

In truth, there is no instruction manual. When we were expecting Gavin, we read tons of parenting books. Many helped. And we received advice from literally everyone we knew, whether asked for or not. Even the friends who'd never had children were somehow experts on child-rearing.

All the advice we received was great.

And all the advice we received was terrible.

Because ultimately, there's no one right way to parent. Yes, I'm saying that right in a parenting book. Apparently.[1]

So, what do we do when it all goes off the rails? How do we keep our cool? How do we handle the *bumps*?

. . . . .

In April, 2020, we'd been hearing a growing drumbeat of bad news. Stories and rumors about an out-of-control virus overseas. I stood outside, in my backyard, playing with the kids. We'd just had a playset installed a few weeks earlier and had recently started working with a fantastic babysitter. The weather was perfect. That gentle spring breeze blew scents of flowers and grass. The kids were laughing. But that thrum of worry couldn't be ignored. My phone buzzed.

And the world shut down.

I remember texting our new babysitter that she would not, in fact, be able to start. I remember how surreal the moment felt—like a car crash, where everything's suddenly slow motion and nothing feels real. Was this really happening? Stay inside? Keep the kids out of school? I'd been through a lot in my life, but nothing had prepared me for this.

Gavin, at the time, attended a wonderful Montessori preschool. Montessori, if you're not familiar with the concept, is a form of education that involves high levels of child-led activities and a large focus on specific physical manipulatives to build early skills. I am definitely a Montessori fan. The only thing Montessori doesn't work well with at all . . . is global pandemics.

When his school shut down, the answer was obvious. I'd been a teacher prior to becoming a stay-at-home dad. I had my fancy education degree and years of teaching experience. And instead of teaching two hundred kids, I'd be working with two—one of whom was only a baby, so she hardly counted.

I took a deep breath on the first day of attempted homeschooling. I could do this.

Gavin smiled at me. He was confused at school closing. He'd heard my wife and I talking about the pandemic, but I don't think he understood. He was four. I was determined to be the best homeschool teacher I could be and make the day as amazing as possible. I couldn't face the fact that the world I wanted for my son wasn't available. I couldn't explain that I was afraid. Afraid of living in isolation. Afraid of the virus. Afraid for my family and for myself. Afraid for the entire planet.

But, I wasn't going to let fear stop me.

I shared a bit of our first game on that day earlier, in Chapter Two. It was a great example of *yes, and*. However, as you'll see, there was a bit more to the story, which ended up leading to one of the biggest bumps I'd ever experienced as a parent.

It started when Gavin put two folding chairs next to each other and then arranged a group of pillows in front of them.

"Get in the rocket," Gavin said.

"Absolutely, Captain."

At once, I said *yes, and*.

Yes, these chairs and pillows were a rocket ship. It didn't matter what I thought they'd be, what they looked like, or what they could have been instead. Gavin placed a brick into the scene, and I accepted it.

And I instantly added a second brick with the word "Captain." With that single word, I added another layer into the scene: our relationship.

Remember those blinders I mentioned in the Adventures chapter? This was me using those. There was no pandemic. No worries. Just one brick at a time. And this intense play session would go on to become a strong anchor.

We both climbed into the chairs and fastened our seatbelts. We were now saying *yes, and* not just with words, but with our actions. Obviously, a rocket has seatbelts, and we need to use them.

"Take us to the moon," demanded Captain Gavin.

Two bricks. I'm the pilot. We're headed to the moon.

Yes, we've been in this memory before—but now that you know the skills, I want to really break it down.

So, there we were. I was doing my best. Yet by this point, those nerves were building again. That fear and worry. In that moment, I was not clinging to an anchor as I should've been. In fact, I was feeling more and more adrift. I remember turning to one of the posters in our playroom, which showed the planets. While he was only in preschool, how long would this pandemic last? Would I be responsible for his entire education?

"I remind you, sir, that the new engines run on song."

"If we sing about the planets, we can—"

"No, the engines started," he interrupted.

Gavin broke my brick. In fact, he broke two of them. The ship had new engines, and they only ran on song. Instead of saying *yes, and,* he instantly rejected those ideas. As a guide, I quickly moved forward, but tucked that song idea in the back of my head for later.

I shook my body and we zoomed into space.

That's about where I left it in chapter two. We sat on those rickety chairs and shook them, making funny noises. Then I made what were supposed to be spaceship braking sounds. Gavin jumped up.

"The moon has lower gravity." Yeah, I tried to slip in teaching where I could. This was homeschooling, after all. "Whoa, look at how we move."

Here, I started to spacewalk around the room. Gavin joined right in.

"Oh no, an alien!" Gavin jumped behind a pillow, hiding.

Another two bricks—there's an alien there, and it's made him scared.

I quickly moved beside Gavin and handed him a block. "The communicator will translate what he's saying." We paused, pretend-listening to the block. *Brick.*

"He's lost his mommy!" said Gavin. *Brick.*

"Look," I pointed to the ceiling. "A trail of space breadcrumbs. It will lead us to his mom."

Gavin lifted the alien, which was a stuffed animal doll. "Come into our ship." He turned to me. "Do we have fuel?"

Ah, here's my chance to bring back that brick from earlier, and teach too.

I smiled. "We need to sing together. To power the ship."

"Sing what?"

"About where we're going."

I pointed to that space poster, and we spent a few minutes writing our song.

"Around the sun, we have fun . . . Mercury, Venus, Earth, and Mars . . . but just you wait, we're not done . . . Jupiter, Saturn, Uranus, and Neptune . . . "

This was amazing.

The intense playtime lasted about an hour. We visited everything from the song, including a walk on the sun with a fireman putting out the flames in our way. We found the alien's mom, and I believe several friends and extended family members too. Somehow, we got everyone home.

I'll never forget that song or the big smiles or the huge hug.

But wait . . . isn't this chapter about bumps? About problems?

. . . . .

Well, even though we'd had an hour of good, the world was still shuttered outside. And the stress within me had abated for a time, only to swell again.

We'd just had an amazing session and had learned a bit about the planets. Yet, I'd only used an hour of time.

What am I supposed to do the rest of the day?

I'd also already used a ton of energy. By now, you're quite familiar with the type of intense energy ten minutes of intense playtime requires. Sustaining that energy for over an hour isn't easy. By this point, we hadn't even made it to lunch.

"What now?" I remember that question he asked, because it was the same thing I'd asked both myself and the world.

"Wait here a minute."

I ran upstairs, grabbed my laptop and quickly set it up. At that point we took a virtual tour of the Louvre, talking about art. We paused for a quick lunch, before then reading a dozen picture books, staging a puppet show, baking a loaf of banana bread from scratch, and engaging in two more improv-based play sessions—no! I still had more time to fill. I grabbed some paper and together we started drafting our own picture book idea.

Evening descended. My wife signed out of work. She'd been watching Gabby while in a series of Zoom meetings. And I'd done my best to be Super Dad.

Or so I thought.

The next morning arrived.

And I was a husk.

A zombie.

Nightmares had kept me up half the night. Nightmares of a world frozen in fear and locked down. Nightmares that I wasn't good enough as a teacher, a husband, or a father. I woke, covered in sweat, only to find the nightmares hadn't abated. They were there, in my heart.

The first day of lockdown, I overdid it.

And the second day, I collapsed.

I put on movies. I tried to cuddle Gavin on the couch. I tried to tell myself that things would be alright. I had hit a bump unlike any other I'd experienced. I didn't think I could do it. I didn't want to do it. I didn't want to play at all or be a teacher—a career I'd already left, after all. I didn't want the world to be locked down.

I'd seen the news reports. The deaths. The sick.

What if we catch it?

What if we die?

This isn't fair!

This isn't the life I want for myself or my kids!

Gavin looked at me and started to sing.

"Around the sun, we have fun . . . Mercury, Venus, Earth, and Mars . . . but just you wait, we're not done . . . Jupiter, Saturn, Uranus, and Neptune . . . "

Right there, in that moment, the anchor technique was born.

I didn't invent it. Gavin did.

He saw me hitting a bump. He saw his father riddled with fear and worry. He saw me struggling. He threw me a lifeline.

Anchors

We've all had bad days. Bad moments. Bad playtimes.

It doesn't matter what you're coping with. The anchor strategy can do wonders. Rooted in principles of acting,[2] this simple technique is transformative and essential. It's your weapon against every bump. And I do mean *every* bump. It will make a huge difference in playtimes, but use these anchors beyond playtime in your daily life. In 2024, I gave a sermon at our church, during which I walked the entire congregation through the basics of discovering one personal anchor and embracing it toward a more optimistic life. Realizing the power of the anchor technique, I began taking it further, coaching other groups about the power this technique had to help overcome obstacles.

It genuinely works. Time and again, it's transformed my life, the lives of people I've coached, and it will transform your life too.

Let's focus on how anchors apply to three scenarios specifically. We're going to zero in on three bumps: the playtime bump, the external bump, and the internal bump. In the story above, during those first two days of lockdown, we hit elements of all three, and I'll show you what I mean.

THE PLAYTIME BUMP

Let's talk first about what to do when playtime derails.

Obviously, the kids are going to break the rules of improv from time to time. As I've said, that's not bad at all. In fact, as a guide, take those moments and use them to really dig into your own improv skills. The kids will do great. They are sponges and quick learners.

However, what do you do when playtime just goes off the rails?

Well, the first step is to clutch that anchor tight.

Try to get things back on track. Add your bricks. Listen close, and say *yes, and*. But . . . well, sometimes it won't work.

Not every playtime is going to go swimmingly. Dory's well-intentioned advice to "just keep swimming" doesn't always work. What if your kid is ill, or just had a bad day? Or what if, with no obvious external reason at all, everything you're trying in intense playtime just is not working?

If you're getting frustrated, the kids are too. Don't forget that they will perfectly mirror your energy. So, pay attention to what you're showing, and if your emotions start to boil, grab that anchor.

It can help to make a fist. Not in anger, but rather imagine yourself literally squeezing a rope tied to that emotional anchor. On one end of the rope is your encouraging memory. As you squeeze those fingers tight, imagine energy flowing from that memory right up your arm and into your heart.

The next thing to do, in playtime, is to admit it's okay to stop. Don't force the playtime to continue if your kid is in a tantrum. There's no point.

And once that playtime pauses, clutch that anchor again. Like Mary, sing a song that makes you happy. Remind yourself that the kids and the joy matter more.

THE EXTERNAL BUMP

There's always something beyond our control. The storm, as I call it, is very real.

As I type these words, Gavin has had a fever for eight days straight. He's ill and it's breaking my heart. He's seen a doctor multiple times and is taking prescribed medicine. Yet, I still feel powerless. Helpless. Adrift.

So I clutch my anchor. I always reach for anchors that happened fairly recently. Today, my anchor is based on an event just from yesterday. I'd taken some time from work to care for Gavin, and we sat at the table playing games. Then I started making jokes. And not good ones, mind you, but truly terrible dad puns that are half humor and half punishment. We laughed; it was his first real laughter in days, and we just laughed and laughed for about thirty minutes.

As I was driving him back to the doctor and he was sobbing, I clutched that anchor. I thought about that laughter and held it close to my heart. As a pharmacist told me he couldn't get Gavin the medicines he needed because of shortages, I clutched that anchor even harder.

It doesn't always work in the moment.

A while back, Gabby threw up while in line to board a flight. Then, once we finally boarded, she threw up a tiny bit more before falling asleep. We had to leave the plane before takeoff and were stranded at the airport. No backup plans, a sick kid, and a growing sense of stress, all at Christmas. Santa nearly didn't make it that year.

Luckily, this bump came after a magical week at Disney. Anchors galore.

I was not at my best. I reached a boiling point when we lost all our luggage and threw a temper tantrum in front of Gavin—a display I'm not proud of. The storm had battered me so severely that the anchor slipped right out of my hand. I just wanted to get my family home, and I was so angry.

I had never done anything like that before. Yet, even when the anchor slips, it's possible to regain it. The anchor and the emotional recall tied to it is a bridge between chaos and clarity. Sometimes we need to let go of the anchor for a few minutes before we realize just how important it really is.

I saw Gavin watching me. Staring at me, with those big, spongy eyes that absorb everything. And I had to sit him down and explain that while what happened to us was bad, Dad hadn't handled it well either.

The key to the external bump: when you can, and as soon as you can, remember your anchor and clutch it.

THE INTERNAL BUMP

There's an overlap between the external and internal storms we face. And often, one can cause or intensify the other. However, some problems really are of our own making. Fears over money or relationships or the future are often grounded less in external facts and more on internal insecurity.

With parenting and child-rearing, these fears manifest most intently in doubts about our own parenting. Remember the first time you took some intense play out of the house to the playground and beyond? Did you feel like everyone else was judging you as a parent? (Pro tip: no one was.)

THE INTERNAL BUMP IS THE STORM WE CREATE.

When I left teaching, my wife and I made a conscious decision. On the one hand, it was the logical choice. As a public school teacher, I worked more hours for far, far less pay than my wife. If one of us was going to stay home, it should be me. Yet culturally, there was a stigma around dads as caregivers. I became depressed. I wasn't bringing in income. I wasn't helping, and all the groups I tried to bring Gavin to as a baby were populated by at-home Moms.

I faced a massive internal bump.

Am I good enough?

This is one of the most often-asked internal questions many of us face. The answer is always yes. Hard stop.

YES. YOU ARE GOOD ENOUGH.

You are a good enough person, parent, spouse, worker, or whatever else you may be wondering. Yet, that voice never goes away, does it? How do we overcome that block that the doubt creates?

Yep, you guessed it. The anchor.

Specifically, the anchor is a memory of a time you felt good. It's proof that you are good. When I started doubting my usefulness as a SAHD, I learned to focus on the positive, intense bonding I had with my son. I learned to cling to my anchor, even before I'd coined the term.

And now, I'm telling you that it does work.

The internal storms will hit, so ready those anchors.

. . . . .

This brings us back to day two of the pandemic lockdown and my three bumps: an external bump (pandemic), an internal bump (pushing myself to exhaustion over being "good enough"), and even a playtime bump (too low-energy to play with Gavin). The anchors helped, but I'll admit, that day sucked. We watched a lot of TV, and I spent most of the day exhausted and wallowing in self-pity and existential dread. I pulled it back together by day three.

Every actor has an off day. Yet, they keep jumping back onstage. It's the same in life, in parenting, in playtime, or in teaching. Just keep going.

Because ultimately, if your anchor slips from you, it'll be there the next day. Or the next. None of us are perfect. That's part of what makes us human. And those storms are never going to stop rolling in. There will be bumps ahead—many bumps.

The day after I initially wrote this page, my wife and daughter were home ill. I sat in my car, waiting to pick up Gavin for his swim lesson. I'd just received an email about work that made me really upset. Rain was literally pummeling the car, beating down with a constant percussive force. And then the car broke down. I got out to get Gavin, and he melted down at the sudden change.

Storms. Damned storms. Everywhere.

They come. They go.

Yet that anchor remains. And it will always be there when you're ready for it.

Every actor has an off day. Yet, they keep jumping back onstage. It's the same in life, in parenting, in playtime, or in teaching. Just keep going.

BOUNDARIES

I already consider myself a playful parent, but I still benefitted from the *yes, and* method described in this book. The method reminds me to be conscientious of my interactions with my children and not to take over playtime too much with my own ideas, something that I was previously guilty of. When I employed the *yes, and* method with my six-year-old son, we went on a fantastic bed-boat journey. We even rescued his older brothers from a parallel universe when they joined in after enthusiastic *yes, and* encouragement from me. As a busy parent, one of the best things about this book is that it taught me how to gently say no without squashing my kids' spirits. To that end, it helps to make sure I'm in the right headspace to play and sometimes that means delaying playtime.

—Sarah Hovorka, author of *Hattie Hates Hugs* and other children's books, and mother of three from California

Sarah knows that *no, but* can be as powerful as *yes, and* when using the Making It Up Method. The gentle *no, but* is a boundary: "I can't play now, but I'll give you ten minutes after my meeting." All kids wrestle with boundaries. This is not a discipline-centered book. There are literally thousands of those out there. Yet, as a parent, I would be remiss if I didn't at least touch on some strategies that might help. Especially because intense, improv-centered playtime is going to push those boundaries. And ideally, the same skills you have already learned can help reinforce those boundaries. You've likely already experienced a few brushes with rules you might not have expected.

Before I dive into some of the ways the Making It Up Method connects to boundaries, I want to mention that there are countless theories about discipline, yet all the books my wife and I have read about discipline boil down to knowing when to maintain and reinforce boundaries. Boundaries aren't bad. Culture wouldn't exist without them. Rules, laws, mores, customs, and norms keep society functioning. Without lane markers on the road, I'd crash my car. And let's face it, all those years of growing up[1] and school have reinforced boundaries.

Such boundary setting begins early in life. "Don't hit." "Don't scream." From the moment the child is born, we are often focused on nos. Then the kid goes to school, where they learn to follow the rules, listen, and accept the teacher's boundaries. One of these boundaries includes learning to color within the lines. This makes sense. By the time we're adults, we drive within the lines, live within the laws, and follow every boundary and expectation. Boundaries are a necessary part of life and need to be reinforced early.

For many, the answer to boundaries is discipline. Discipline is a form of directed *no,* intended to teach. For example, hit your sibling and get a time-out. Throw a pencil in class and get a call to Mom. Color outside the lines in every assignment and receive a poor grade.

Discipline is not a dirty word. However:

1. **Never hit your kids.** Ever. Just don't. There's a ton of science. But beyond the science, just don't.
2. **Consistency is king.** Especially when it comes to improv-based parenting boundaries. The playtimes are going to be different every time. One playtime might be on Mars, the next under the sea. In one playtime, you might be a hero, in another a villain. However, daily playtime of ten minutes using these strategies is consistency in itself. Remember, the kids will absorb your energy as well. Consistently using an anchor to focus on positive energy creates a positive consistency as well.
3. **If it's not working, switch something up.**

That last one is especially in regard to discipline methods. There are a lot of discipline methods out there—often billed in books as "this method is best, ignore the rest." That's great for selling books, but not always great for kids. If you're trying something and it isn't working, try something else. Rachel and I like books that focus on positive rewards and incentives, but even these have not always been successful.

So let's talk about coloring in the lines, using Making It Up.

Remember, there are rules. As a quick refresher:

1. Say *yes, and.*
2. Say *no, but.*
3. Keep adding.
4. Avoid questions.
5. Don't break the bricks.
6. Stay in the moment.
7. Be specific.
8. Toys are not necessarily your friends.
9. Don't plan ahead!
10. Go big!
11. Always carry your anchor.

These eleven rules are the foundation of the improv part of your intense playtimes. They're also handy to recall when setting boundaries for play and beyond, to avoid some bumps. Don't forget that the rules of Making It Up are guidelines to succeed in creating more intense and meaningful experiences. In a similar vein, your boundaries should do the same.

Physical Boundaries

I will never forget the first time I saw Gavin. I could be all poetic and say it was this magical, Hollywood moment where the stars twinkled and the angels sang. That's bull, though. The truth is it was disgusting. I mean, let's be honest. Human births are really gross. Gavin emerged as this gangly, bloody mess. My wife and I were exhausted and stressed. Rachel, of course, had the far harder job, and tons of pain.

And yet, it's in that weird, tiring, disgusting moment when we first become parents that our priorities and responsibilities shift forever. From that moment on, the single biggest priority is your kid's welfare. So obviously all boundaries, and any discussion of rules, need to center on the safety of all.

Imagine you're in the middle of an intense Making It Up session, and little Johnny lifts a real baseball bat. "This is my sword," he says. Then he proceeds to whack you in the legs. Nope. Not safe.

Obviously, we're not going to allow hitting. Yet, how can you say *yes, and* to an unsafe brick? Do you instantly have to stop the playtime?

If safety is an immediate concern, *yes,* stop, *and* get to a place of safety first. Safety always comes first. That said, the more you engage in intense, improv-based playtimes, remembering that you're a guide and not an equal, the quicker you're going to become at picking up tricks to keep the play going.

"This is my sword," says Johnny.

"Safety Police," you shout in a robot voice. "Your sword is now confiscated for the Museum of Safety."

Yes, as corny as it sounds, "Safety Police" can often work. Or sometimes you can just distract by introducing another completely opposite brick. Remember, it's okay to stop if someone is really in harm's way. Safety always comes first.

Emotional Boundaries

This is a bit trickier than physical safety, but it is just as important. Emotional boundaries create and maintain safety just as physical boundaries do. Sticks and stones can break bones, but names can be just as hurtful. Make sure that everyone is comfortable during playtime. This can include topics. My family is vegan, for instance, and Gavin once got upset when a friend tried to pretend play butcher shop with him. Emotional boundaries are important.

Another boundary to watch out for is dynamics among kids when dealing with larger groups. Are the kids all ignoring one kid? Are they picking repeatedly on one person? Are they pairing into bullies and victims every playtime? These are unsafe patterns emotionally and must be stopped. It's completely appropriate as an adult to step in and change those patterns, ensuring everyone's emotional boundaries are respected.

With emotional boundaries, watch for signs of discomfort. If someone winces when a brick is introduced, it's okay to pivot. Don't cling to a toxic brick. In a similar vein, if the dynamics of play feel off or toxic, switch it up and remedy the situation. Stop the play if necessary. Or redirect. You're the guide.

End Times and Transitions

Cards on the table, 90 percent of tricky behavior I've seen in young kids comes at one of three times. The first is when a kid is hungry. Kids learn hunger from birth. Usually, the tactic when hungry is to scream until food arrives. That approach never fully changes. And I'll admit, even as an adult, I get cranky when I'm hungry. The second tricky time for young kids comes when they have to potty. This isn't even related to potty training. Kids can be fully potty trained for years, but if there's a poop building up, their behavior may be off. The third tricky time is transition time. Transitions are going to impact intense play a lot.

Transitions are tough for a lot of kids—and a lot of adults. As you move in and out of playtime sessions, consider using a specific signal. A handclap, for instance. Or, if you'd like to be theatrical, announce, "Lights up!" to mark the beginning of play and call, "Curtain," when it's over. There's a chance transitions can get dicey. Be prepared. And be patient.

Many kids benefit from a warning, leading up to a change. Perhaps a one-minute timer before playtime starts and a separate timer for when it ends. Give that one-minute announcement, and then another ten-second announcement if necessary. Many kids will also benefit from having playtime at the same general time each day. If you can build the intense playtime into your schedule or larger routine at a consistent time, do so.

Interruptions

No one wants to be interrupted. But life happens.

Remember way back in chapter one, I introduced the idea of *yes, and* and paired it with *no, but*. The *no, but* idea centers around no interruptions, but only when you're ready. Try to hold to that. No phones, no screens, no work. However, at times an interruption will happen. The doorbell rings and it's an emergency. The power goes out. A group of actual aliens climb out of their UFO on your lawn. Or, maybe the kid starts throwing up. Who knows!

Interruptions are actually forced transitions. There's no time to prepare, no time to adjust. Patience is key in these moments. Stay calm and remember the sponge-like nature of kids. If an interruption causes you stress, they'll be stressed too. Interruptions are great places to grab those anchors tightly.

. . . . .

Let's look at a playtime together. I'm going to break down what's going on, but there's going to be some real boundary pushing and rule breaking here. This is playtime between Tony and his son, Nate, who is five.

Tony: [Claps his hands.] Light's up.

(Tony knows that Nate needs some help with transitions. They've decided that a handclap and announcement at the beginning of intense playtime helped Nate know that the fun's beginning. This is also Tony's signal that he is interruption-free, leaving the phone off and on silent, with ten minutes fully devoted to Nate.)

Nate: [Makes dinosaur-style body motions.] Rrrrroarrr!

Tony: Tyrannosaurus Bob, I'm afraid you'll have to wait for recess. Sit down and turn to page eighty-five in your math book.

(Tony accepted Nate's brick of being a dinosaur, specifically a T-Rex. He added the name Bob. He also added a brick that he's a teacher, and they're both in school.)

Nate: Grrrrr. [Sits.] I ate my math book. [Grins wide.] And I'm still hungry.

(Nate accepted his dad's bricks, and the play is building nicely. They're at school, he's eaten the math book, he's still hungry.)

Tony: [Holds hands up in exaggerated shock, and then pretends to flip through an imaginary chart.] Not again! Tyrannosaurus Bob, how many times do I have to remind you that you're allergic to numbers!

Nate: [Throws himself on the ground, rolling to one side.] Math . . . it hurts . . . oh, help!

Tony: [Using an imaginary phone with his hand.] Nurse Pachycephalosaurus, I need you down here right away. Bob swallowed math again.

Nate: I'm still hungry! [Pretends to chew.] I ate the other students. Buuuurp!

(The play has been building really well. Both Tony and Nate are adding bricks and accepting each other's ideas. Tony has followed his improv rules well. He's continuously adding, going big when he can, and avoiding toys and questions. He's staying in the moment and being specific. He's also not planned any of this. He's open to seeing where the play will go.)

Tony: [Moves to other side of the playroom and changes body positions, his head now far forward. He speaks in a high, nasal voice.] Nurse Pachycephalosaurus is here, as requested. Oh, Bob, you ate your class. Again. Third time this week.

Nate: [Jumps up.] No, I'm the nurse!

(Nate has broken his dad's bricks here. Yet, everything up to this point has been going great. Tony is a guide and knows that if he insists on remaining the nurse, it could become confrontational and disrupt the entire play session. Instead, he quickly moves back to the persona of the teacher. Note, that the teacher was never defined in the play. Is it another dino? A human? While undefined, Tony chooses to play it the way he did earlier.)

Tony: Oh thank you for coming so quickly, Nurse. [He points to the floor.] Bob just ate math, and the entire class. He might have even added the students while eating them, which makes his hives worse.

Nate: [Grabs a toy dino and throws it on ground to be "Bob."] Bad Bob. [Kicks the dino. Then pauses a moment.] No, Dad, you be Bob.

(Play is hitting some rough moments. Nate's starting to lose focus and isn't building bricks. We've hit a bump in the playtime, but Tony's still hoping it's a small bump. After all, a little recasting might be fine, if they can get playtime back on track. Tony lays down and groans.)

Tony: Ohhhh, my belly. That class hurts inside. And I'm still hungry, Nurse.

Nate: [Leans down.] Well, I'm gonna have to saw you open to get the class out.

Tony: That makes sense. I hope they're not mad like they were last time.

(Well it's a bit dark, but playtime's back on track. Tony's back to accepting bricks and building the play. Tony is also accepting and building. Remember, the core skill in playtime always comes back to yes, and.)

Nate: [Holds hand like a saw and then hits Tony hard in the chest.]

(Hitting is definitely not allowed in Tony's house. Yet, he's invested in the play. Tony needs a way to let Nate know that he crossed a boundary with his unsafe behavior. Tony decides to pause the play.)

Tony: Pause. That hurt. Hitting is not allowed.

Nate: I cut you open!

Tony: Say that you're sorry, and we can unpause.

Nate: Sorry.

Tony: Unpause. Hey, there goes all the class, they all came out.

Nate: [Lowers head, like a pachycephalosaurus, the headbutting dino.] Get back in your seats, class! [Slams head into Tony.]

We'll pause the above scene. With two unsafe behaviors in a row, the playtime is going off the rails.

IT'S OKAY TO STOP IF IT'S NOT WORKING.

And what to do about those unsafe behaviors?

I'll be honest. There are thousands of books on discipline out there, and we've been through hundreds of them in my house, but it's still a struggle. My children are perfect little angels . . . except when they're not. We focus on rewards; we focus on consistency. We use the loss of things they like, such as tablet time, as consequences. Does it work? Well, not always.

That's where the anchors come in.

Even as I type, I had a terrible day. Gabby had six enormous tantrums today, all related to potty use. It was terrible. Not gonna lie, I had to walk away more than once just to calm myself down. And that's okay. Respect your own emotional health too.

What kept me going?

My anchor.

It genuinely helps.

At our church, I gave a speech about radical optimism. As I looked out at the congregation, I saw a lot of anxiety, fear, and stress. I walked them through a quick guided meditation and proceeded to introduce the anchor. Then I pivoted, asking everyone to use an anchor to embrace optimism. That's what the anchor really provides: not just emotional recall, but radical optimism when the storm is unbearable. For weeks after giving the sermon, congregants approached me saying that their entire outlook on life felt different. Five months later, I found myself giving a similar speech for TEDx in Philadelphia, and again I walked the crowd through stress to a point of choosing joy. The anchor technique is a powerful and life-changing tool. It is also a parent's lifeline during rough behavior from the kids.

There's one final note for using these skills when kids approach boundaries. Try *yes, and*. Part of being an adult, especially a parent, is a sort of built-in, innate need to constantly say no. While a lot of time the answer to whatever the kids are newly begging for is "no," approaching the mentality of trying a "yes, and" when boundaries are approached can be remarkably different and effective.

For example, Gavin wanted to play a game he'd heard about. Except we don't own any gaming system, and the game isn't available on his tablet. He begged for this game, and I finally agreed to download it on my phone.

Now this might not seem like a big deal, and really, it isn't. Yet I have to confess, the original thought of him borrowing my phone bugged me. Phones are part of us. My phone is mine. I don't want him accidentally emailing my agent or deleting something I need or dropping the phone and breaking it. In short, I didn't fully trust him. I was conditioned to say no.

But instead, I tried a *yes, and.*

Yes, and I'll set a timer.

I added a boundary of my own.

And guess what? It was no big deal at all. I remember letting him play the game (*Pokémon Go*) at a playground with a friend. The friend's mom looked at me and said, "You let him borrow your phone? I'd never do that. You are very brave."

Maybe I am. Or maybe I'm just realizing that the power of *yes, and* isn't limited to playtime. We still have our boundaries, but I was able to recognize that mine didn't have to be as limited as my gut initially said.

One of my favorite episodes of *Bluey* is from the third season. In the episode "Pavlova," Bingo asks for some pavlova. Her mum says no. She encourages Bingo to try some edamame instead. A boundary is marked. No dessert. Try something healthy. However, Bluey then embarks on an elaborate improv to break this rule. The episode is quite funny, but the core idea is interesting. Bandit sees a boundary being pushed. He could step in and say no to his girls trying to get the dessert they've already been told they can't have. Instead, he jumps right into improv-mode. As part of the playtime, he acts big, says *yes, and,* and engages with the girls in a fun, entertaining way. In the end, he even gives in and lets Bingo have the pavlova. For a moment, you wonder if he simply gave in to all the pushing against boundaries the girls tried. But then Bingo tries edamame, something she wasn't willing to do just ten minutes earlier. He might have bent the boundary around dessert first, but in doing so, he engaged Bingo in trying something new.

It's not always going to be that simple.

It's not always going to be fun.

Boundaries exist and will be tested.

Parenting is not going to be 100 percent joyful every minute of every day. Yet by keeping to routines, listening carefully, and clutching that anchor, boundaries can be maintained and respected even in the most boundary-pushing playtimes.

Keep in mind that the more intense playtimes you have, the better you'll become at recognizing how to enforce and maintain boundaries while keeping the play building and fun. And the more often you use the anchor technique, the more radically it will start to alter your daily thinking. In addition, the more often you try saying *yes, and* to a slight boundary push, the more you'll realize your own limits might be more adjustable than you'd first considered.

ONE SIZE DOESN'T FIT ALL

Daily interaction with their parents, especially during special playtime, profoundly impacts a child's development; consistent engagement and positive reinforcement foster trust, emotional resilience, and a deep sense of security.

—Alisha Fletcher, social worker and mother of four, from Delaware

As a social worker, Alisha knows the power of daily play. Ten minutes a day can transform your relationship. However, it's key to realize that every child is unique. During my years as a teacher I worked with many children, encountering kids with different needs and personalities. I have neurodiverse family members and close friends with special needs. Simply put, one size *never* fits all.

This is true regarding all parenting books and techniques. Take what works for your kid, but be ready to adjust. There is no expert out there who knows your kid, or the kids you work with, better than you do.

The fun thing with Making It Up is that it is uniquely suited to reach kids with special needs in a meaningful and engaging way. Theatre incorporates body, voice, and imagination in a way that is unique and liberating for many.

One student I recall as being particularly strong in my theatre class was deaf. He arrived in my class with an ASL interpreter. Instantly, I felt nervous. How would I communicate to this student when I didn't know sign language? And how would a class that was so rooted in communication work via an interpreter?

Fast forward to the final day of school, he was teary-eyed, giving me a handshake before handing me a card he'd written telling me that the class wasn't just his favorite—it had literally changed his entire high school experience. Theatre and improv had given him the confidence to be himself and explore interactions in a way he'd never before encountered.

Theatre is a form of communication that can break barriers. For many, it is liberating. For others, it is a powerful way to see playtime differently. Many neurodiverse children communicate and interpret the world through a different lens. Playtime isn't just about imagination; it's a way to process the world.

One growing field that specifically bridges theatre with neurodivergence is drama therapy. Trained drama therapists incorporate theatre skills with neurodiverse children to bring about significant therapeutic change. In other words, theatre doesn't just improve playtime or the bonds between adults and kids, theatre can actually help heal. In one study of drama therapies being used to help kids with autism or social anxieties, the use of theatre was shown to reduce anxiety and directly decrease psychosocial issues.[1] The skills in this book might seem like fun and games, and they are, but they can also drastically change lives.

Listen with Ears and Eyes

The key to the Making It Up Method, especially when interacting with children who are neurodiverse, is flexibility. The role of guide is even stronger. Keep using those improv skills as you pay special attention to everything the child says and does.

For autistic children particularly, it sometimes helps to slow down the speed with which you add bricks to playtime. Bricks will come. Both from the kids and you, but sometimes you have to listen a little harder or focus a little more on the means that the kids are using to communicate. Are they using their body to convey a brick? Use your eyes along with your ears to listen and see what the kid is adding. Communication doesn't have to be verbal, and neither do bricks. A hand outstretched might be offering you something, a fist raised Superman-style might mean flying, and so on.

It's also critical to observe how invested the child actually is in playtime. With autistic and other neurodiverse children, giving a little extra time to get into the play can really help. Also, don't stress if they can't make it a full ten minutes. Five or six minutes of intense playtime can still be hugely impactful, especially if done daily. Observe intently throughout, and you'll start to notice when the kid wants more and when they want less. They are a sponge to your energy, but you need to be a similar-style sponge to their needs. Do they need you to be extra slow? Extra silly? The body cues and responses from the kid you're engaged with will dictate those answers, and they will vary every playtime.

At its core, all of the skills in this book center on connection. Everything else is secondary. Think of the bond you're forming with the kid as the trunk of a tree. Everything else—the extra rules and techniques and so on—are the branches and leaves. Your anchor provides the roots. Don't worry about those branches and leaves until your roots are firm and your trunk is strong.

The key with children who have special needs is to really zero in on *yes, and* as well as your anchor. Saying *yes, and* can be especially empowering to kids who are used to hearing no. Children with Oppositional Defiant Disorder or ADHD, for example, might have encountered a lot of nos from their parents, teachers, and peers. Obviously, boundaries and safety are paramount, but during the ten minutes of intense play, try focusing on the *yes* phase as much as possible. The kids will see that, within the bounds of playtime, positive play brings constant validation.

In fact, the very nature of the daily ten-minute playtime is similar to the concept of Parent Child Interaction Therapy, or PCIT. PCIT is a common method used by psychologists to help children and parents. We've done PCIT ourselves, as mentioned in an earlier chapter. Although PCIT is a different process than this book advocates, it's similar in its focus on daily, intense playtime as a means to bond with and connect to children. The simple act of setting aside ten minutes daily to solely be a parent can be life-changing.

Perhaps the greatest research has been done connecting autism-spectrum disorders to theatre. Olivia Rhodes, a researcher at Eastern Michigan University, writes, "Daily intensive exposure to drama and theatre can be a viable option to promote the development of social skills among children on the autism spectrum. The activities seemed to promote particular gains in caregiver/peer interaction, adjusting to routines, eye contact, and social perceptions/cues."[2] Rhodes wrote this sentiment after observing kids who attended a single week of an intense theatre-focused camp. Theatre has the power to transform interactions, including those between adults and children, or caregivers and children, in only a week! That's astounding. A single week of intense playtime, centered around theatre produced quantifiable results in both children and adults.

Which brings the question, what results are you seeing so far? Have you been noticing them? Let's take a moment to consider.

In the table below, jot down some of what you have experienced. Talk about the types of playtimes you were having before starting. Have they changed? How? And what are you hoping happens next? Try to list at least three things for each.

BEFORE I STARTED THE BOOK	AT THIS POINT	WHERE I HOPE TO GO
1.	1.	1.
2.	2.	2.
3.	3.	3.

Next, I want you to consider the kids. Either your children or the ones you're working with if you are a teacher or caregiver. Are the children experiencing any unique or specific needs in intense playtime? Are you encountering the same problems repeatedly?

Jot them down here, so that you can focus on these as I offer some potential solutions.

CONCERNS:

Moving Closer to Your Goals

Not every solution will fit every child. But you've already come far. Look at that progress table above. Hopefully, you're experiencing new and intense playtimes, and are bonding with your kids in a way that's stronger than ever before. Also pay attention to that goal column. How can we move toward that? Here are some tips.

1. **Split the play:** Since the first chapter, I've advocated that ten minutes of intense play is central to building the bond. That remains true. However, it doesn't have to be a single, continuous improvisation. If ten minutes is too long, try breaking it into two five-minute blocks. Ideally these should be back-to-back, but after the first five minutes, chuck all the bricks and start a new game. This will work for some kids who might have trouble with longer attention and focus.
2. **Toys and props:** In chapter three, I mentioned avoiding toys if possible. For some kids, toys and props might help to maintain the playtime. Before diving into character-based toys such as action figures, consider generic things. Paper towel rolls or plastic cups make fantastic props, for example, and can become anything. If brick building isn't going as smoothly as you'd hoped, try a prop.

3. **New environment:** Just as I encouraged you to take the play outside, for some kids playing in a new environment can be huge in itself. If the living room is associated with watching TV, for instance, the kid might not feel comfortable playing in a theatrical way there. Try going outside, or to a different room. Sometimes a change of environment can make a difference.
4. **Soundscape:** For some kids, putting music on in the background can be a helpful way to enhance playtime. Keep in mind, for others this might be too stimulating. For some, however, it might help a lot. Try creating a playlist of soundtrack-style music, preferably without lyrics. Then play the music during the intense play and try to match your emotions and energy to the tempo and energy of the music. In addition to augmenting the playtime, it is a nice, clear signal of when playtime begins and ends.
5. **Focus on one at a time:** I haven't talked about multiple kids and groups yet (it's coming), but at this point if you've been doing your intense playtimes with more than one kid at once, you might not be seeing the results you're hoping for. Try focusing on only one child at a time, and see if it makes a difference.

. . . . .

Hopefully by now you see that one size really doesn't fit all. These methods work, but you might need to tweak them to fit your child's needs. Every child is unique, and every child learns in a unique manner. Yet, theatre can transform any relationship.

In fact, theatre can transform lives, and I know this firsthand.

In 2010, I was studying to become a theatre teacher. I worked days as a long-term high school substitute teacher, teaching science. In the afternoons and evenings, I helped with the school play, designing the set and coaching the actors in an assistant role to their teacher. The school was putting on a performance of *Scapino!* A retelling of the commedia dell'arte play *Scapin* by Molière.

One of the kids in my science class was a boy named Edwin. To be honest, I didn't love teaching science. It wasn't a field I knew particularly well, and I was doing my best to teach from the guide and curriculum until the class's main teacher returned from maternity leave. I was, in many ways, just a placeholder.

I did, however, love helping in the theatre program. *Scapino!* was my first stage design. I created a ramp-based set that I thought looked really good. We had a fantastic, fun group of kids with an intense energy that I knew from my own years as a high school actor and would later cherish as a theatre teacher. The one thing *Scapino!* lacked was male leads. We didn't have nearly enough guys for the play.

I'd mentioned the upcoming auditions in my science class. And then . . . I started nudging Edwin. I don't recall exactly why. I remember Edwin seemed a bit lost as a student. He was a senior in my sophomore science class struggling to pass his classes. Edwin was distracted, perhaps a bit troubled, but clearly bright. Maybe something was going on outside of school? I nudged him a bit harder to audition. And he did.

Edwin was cast in a leading role. After school, he would transform into this energized, excited kid. His eyes lit up in a way I'd never seen in class. Yet, I hadn't realized the true impact until he gave a speech before opening night. Edwin stood before the cast, tears in his eyes, thanking everyone involved. Then he started telling a story. A story about a kid who'd been mixed up in gangs and spent time in juvie. A kid who would be right back on the streets if he hadn't auditioned for a show. Today, Edwin is a successful actor, DJ, and musician, as well as the CEO of his own recording label. He's performed on the West and East Coast, including at major sports arenas. And this is just the beginning for him.

Theatre transformed Edwin's life.

THEATRE CAN TRANSFORM *ANY* LIFE.

I mention Edwin in this chapter about different needs because he's the perfect example of the iceberg analogy all kids represent. We work with children and we think we know everything about them, but even when they are our own kids, we never fully know everything going on under the surface.

Children are complex, layered individuals. A stressful event you forgot about can prompt issues a month later. And neurodivergent kids go even further. They process the world differently. They process emotions differently.

As you engage in intense theatre-based play, know that you are making a difference. It might not seem like it in the moment. You might have to split

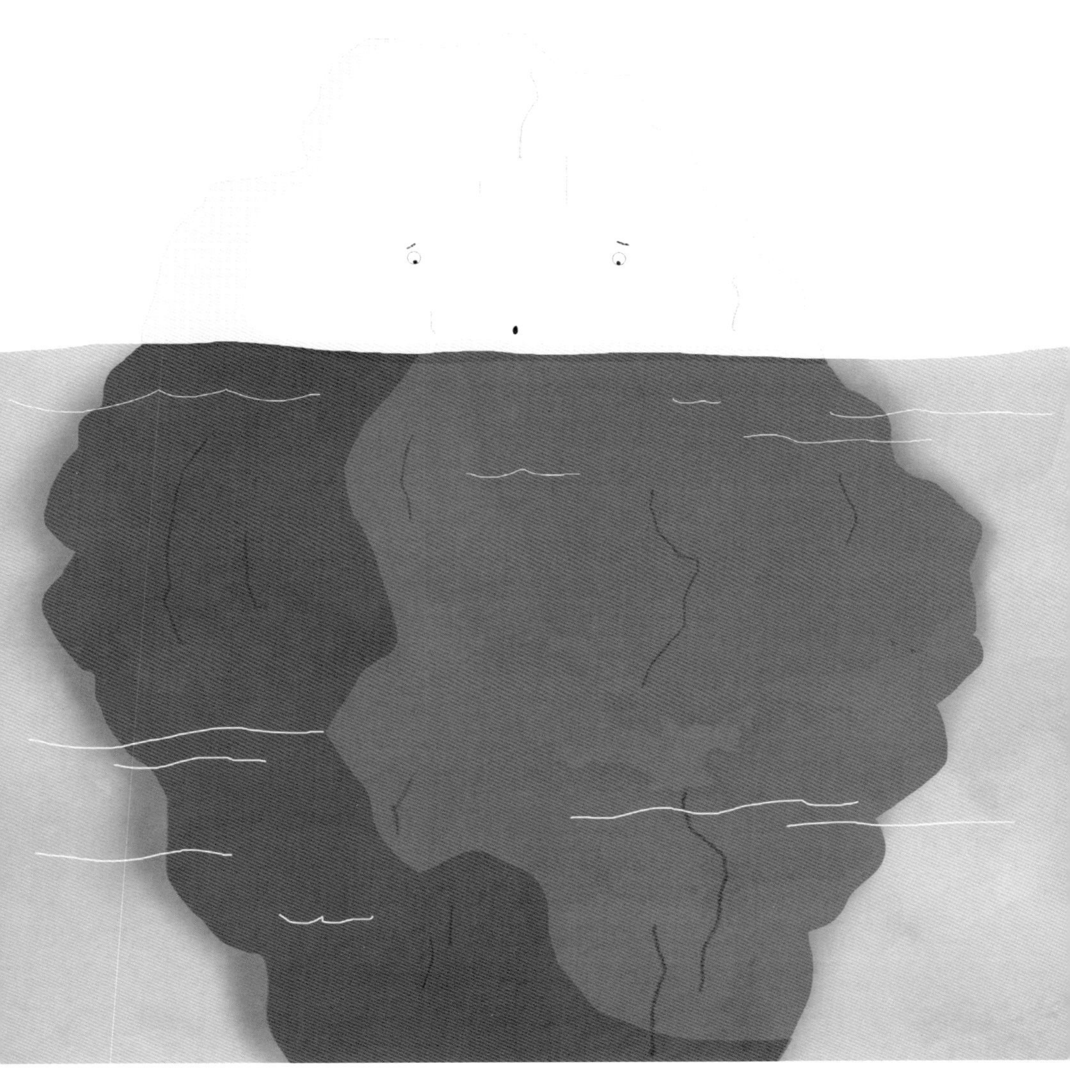

the play, or even abandon the play for that day. Yet every time you try, your connection is growing stronger.

And who knows how drastically your life and the child's life might change as a result of those connections.

Whether the kid you're working with has struggled with emotional issues, failing grades, or even legal troubles. Theatre skills can change the course.

If the kid is neurodivergent or neurotypical. If the kid is straight or LGBTQIA+. If the kid is happy or sad. One size doesn't fit all, but the skills do make a difference for everyone.

I hope this book helps more Edwins out there. It's one of the main reasons I set out to write it. I genuinely want to change lives, and these skills can help. Speaking of Edwin, and high schoolers, let's take a closer look in the next chapter at older kids.

OLDER KIDS

With two teens and two tots, my wife and I are constantly seeking ways to better connect with them. In *Making It Up*, Chris Mannino shares the secret sauce to fostering meaningful ways to interact with and inspire young children: improvisation. As I dove into the opening pages, I found myself wanting to try his simple yet powerful techniques, such as *yes, and,* with my children right away. I did so as they passed by, catching them off guard with my improvisation. But they naturally caught on and soon we were engaged in spontaneous banter and play. The best thing about this approach is it can be used anytime, anywhere, with no special tools or training outside of one's imagination. And it even worked with the teens. I asked them to join us for improv. After the usual rolling of the eyes, they started to get into it. Now they sometimes do it on their own with the two younger ones, which keeps both sets of kids busy and active.

—Richard Lin, author and stay-at-home dad of four, from Oregon

Richard recognized that improvisation isn't just a game-changer for his young kids. It can work wonders on relationships with teenagers and older kids as well. While we've focused on younger kids so far, those children grow up fast. Many have older siblings or friends. While it might seem that tweens and teens are a bit too old to engage in playtime, with some twists, these techniques still work.

As Edwin and countless other students I've worked with prove, theatre can be transformative at any age. It's helping you to transform as you read this book. Yet, applying the skills in this book will be different as you work with older kids. While I would love to go dragonhunting and freeze ray shopping with my kids well into their teenage years, I'm not so naïve as to expect that will occur forever.

So, how can we incorporate the skills from this book to include older kids?

I'm going to break this down into two parts. First, let's look at the older siblings when there are still young kids present (this will tie into the group dynamics in the following chapter, but it is a bit unique as well), and then we'll look at skills from this book when there are no young kids present.

The Big Sibling Guides

Perhaps you are having intense playtimes with younger kids, but you also have an older kid in the house. Everything in this book applies as written: you should be focused on those improv skills, using your anchor, and building relationships with the younger kids brick by brick.

While you're doing that, use these new techniques as an opportunity to strengthen your bond with the older kids. Get them in on the fun. "This is a new way we're going to play with your brother," or "Hey, can you help me teach this new trick with your sister?" The level of involvement is going to vary kid to kid, but getting them in as guide is going to make playtime more fun for your littlest while also giving you a unique chance to bond with your older one.

There's a ton of variation in families. You may have stepchildren, a ten-year age gap, a five-year age gap, and on and on . . . . Yet, you should have enough of a handle on the techniques in this book to include another player. Maybe this technique can be their newest side quest. Many older siblings I've met and taught love teaching their little siblings new things. And for those older siblings who might not be the fondest of tea parties or quests, this is the perfect way to pump some energy and excitement back into the playtimes.

PLAY WITH BOTH. PLAY WITH ALL.

During the pandemic, my wife and I would end many nights with a family run around our house using loud music, silly motions, and chasing imaginary creatures. All four of us interacting in a high energy, intense way helped us stave off the cabin fever that accompanied the lockdowns, and it was a great way to bond as a family as well.

It's also good to encourage the older kids to become their own guides and play one-on-one with the younger kids. I'm reminded of the "Santa's Helper" technique. Basically, this concept is what many families we know do around Santa Claus. Yes, my family, like millions of others, spends every December lying to our children about a mythical being named Santa. This magical man appears overnight on Christmas Eve, leaving gifts.

Except . . . he doesn't. Obviously, it's the parents. Same for the Tooth Fairy, the Easter Bunny, and any other similar tradition. The Santa's Helper idea is that when a kid learns the truth, you face a crisis. Have they lost faith in you? Have they lost faith in the wider world? What about all those movies, TV shows, and songs? Reality is a bit shaky for a few minutes. So, you explain that they've been invited to participate in the magic and help spread the spirit to their younger siblings. They can help you pick or wrap gifts and continue to talk up the myth.

I'll admit, I think Santa's fun. But I also think hunting dragons in the woods is fun. They're along the same level of reality. And maybe that's why the Santa's Helper model works so well with improv-based play for older siblings. Theatre is, in essence, a form of lying. A form of pretend and make-believe that we accept for the duration of the play. And just as it's okay to say Santa brought those toys, it's also okay to say that you are on the moon, or underwater, or on the back of a griffin during playtime. The more the older kids help out, the more the magic of intense playtime becomes real for all.

TEENS AND ANCHORS

I'm obviously a big proponent of the anchor technique. Yet, as much as it's helped you, it can help an older child such as a teenager even more. Why? Because at its heart, the anchor technique is no more and no less than emotional regulation. Let's be honest, the teenage years can be riddled with storms.

I'm not advocating anchors as an alternative to therapy. If you have a child or are working with a child who has severe emotional needs, or thoughts of self-harm, they need professional help. Therapists save lives, and this cannot be overstated.

Yet, for kids simply overburdened with school, puberty, peers, social media, and the adolescent storms of life, the anchor technique can make a big difference. If you have a kid who you think might benefit from the anchor technique, try this method to teach them:

First, sit down with no distractions. Cell phones away. Laptop off. If this is too hard to do in the house, try asking them to take a walk while you talk. They might think they're in trouble, but having no distractions is key.

Next, talk out a memory that you two have shared. Something you know brought them great joy. Maybe a vacation, or an achievement at school. It's likely no surprise that in my teen years, the most special memories often occurred around school plays and musical performances.

Finally, encourage them to remember that feeling, and to think about that moment the next time things get crazy or frustrating. Tell them it's a little tip to draw their attention somewhere concrete. If they're curious for more details, loan them this book, but don't push too hard. Then, the next time you notice them dealing with a storm, mention that same memory again. Each time you see them struggling, keep reminding them about the anchor memory, or a similar one. Chances are the technique will stick, even without concretely teaching it or reading about it.

THE BRICK-SHARERS

For many parents, there is a natural progression of letting go. The first years are intense, and full of young children with constant energy and connection. By adolescence, young adults are no longer little kids. They are their own people, seeking independence and their own lives. Often, a gulf grows between parent and child that is a natural evolution of simply growing up.

Yet, this gulf can seem insurmountable at times. The relationship between parent and child has changed, and that's not always for the better. For some parents, this period can be a phase of distancing. How, then, can you use the skills in this book to help reinforce this changing relationship? How can you build a bridge over the growing gulf?

The concept of bricks, rooted in improv and theatre, is an idea that transcends age. At its core, the brick is an idea. And the play advocated throughout this book is built by accepting and adding ideas. This foundational skill can be used in any relationship, including with adolescents.

As opposed to focusing solely on unstructured and spontaneous play, focus on accepting an idea. Bear in mind that at this phase of psychosocial development, kids crave acceptance—acceptance from themselves, their peers, and yes, even their parents. What stronger way to validate a growing teenager who's shaping a new identity than with *yes, and*?

This can work in one of two ways. Ideally, they'll throw an idea at you. This can be anything from "Can I have a popsicle?" or "Pizza tonight?" to "Let's plant a garden" or "I want a mohawk." As in the early chapters, the natural response to many of these suggestions is to say no. And obviously use your judgement and keep safety in mind. Yet, at some point, there will be a brick thrown out there you never imagined saying yes to. Now try saying *yes, and* too. "You can get a mohawk, and I'll get one too." (Why not? Go for it!)

Accepting your adolescent's idea and adding on can open a bridge across that widening gulf. It will give you something to talk about. Something to connect over. And the more you start to connect, the more you build (*keep adding*). The crazier you go with things, the stronger the connection—so yeah, get that mohawk yourself (*go big*). And the more time you spend with them, without distractions like phones, the stronger that bond becomes.

The other way the brick building technique can work is to throw a brick out yourself initially. This is helpful for the kids who are more insular, or who make no move to communicate with you, or who you can't reach except via text. If your kid isn't listening to you and you're not connecting, try doing something different to get their attention. Make sure you offer something that you are willing to give. Don't offer a popsicle and then demand they eat their broccoli first. That's smashing your own brick. Yes, it could backfire (Oh man, did Dad really think we'd want to go camping?), or it could massively succeed (The best part was when Dad took us camping). But you'll never know until you try. Once you've made contact and broken through that initial barrier, the bricks will come. Be *listening* for when they add one, and then instantly say *yes, and*.

A special note: This is the time of life when it's important to be receptive to identity. Kids are coming out as LGBTQIA+ or are forming new identities around faith or politics. Those identities might not align with your ideas or expectations, but the strongest, most powerful thing you can do is say *yes, and*. Show them acceptance, and build on that acceptance together.

Drama as Community

We've talked about theatre skills in this the book a lot, and how incorporating those skills can change any relationship. Hopefully you're seeing the ways this applies to older kids as well, but there's one more big way drama can help. Just as theatre changed Edwin's life, drama can become a source of community.

Not everyone is going to be interested in helping out with a school play or auditioning to be on stage, but it's important to note how vastly varied the theatre community can be. Putting on a production, such as an after-school production, involves many kids who never step onstage. As theatre teachers, we needed volunteer students in every aspect. Maybe one kid would want to learn to operate lights? Maybe another would want to help paint scenery? Set building involves construction skills and is a favorite for kids who like to create useable housing, including walls, steps, and doors. And for those who just want a small taste, working the theatre lobby is an easy way to dip your toes in with smaller time commitment.

The key to all of these is the community. Just as you've been building bonds with your kids, the theatre world allows kids to build new relationships with their peer groups. This is especially helpful for introverted kids who might not feel that they fit in with typical crowds. I had many, many students who wanted friends, but didn't know how to make them. After joining just one show, they'd tell me that they'd made new friends for life. It's a powerful sense of community.

TIPS TO HELP YOUR CHILD FIND COMMUNITY IN THEATRE:

Tip 1: If you think your kid could benefit from theatre but know they'll push back on a suggestion from Mom or Dad, try to think of ways to encourage indirectly. Leave flyers around they just happen to find. Or elicit the help of one of the kid's friends or teachers. I only tried out for my first middle school play because my best friend bet me that he'd get a bigger role. Peer pressure can be an ally, in this case. And again, this isn't for all. If they're not interested, don't force it.

Tip 2: You can join the community with your kid and build the bond even more. Again, thinking of school performances, adult volunteers can be a huge help. Ask the drama teacher what they need and how you can help. Spending time working on the same show, as part of the same new community, will strengthen the bond between you and your kid in amazing ways. I had many parents of students who would come and help for a time, and they were happy to share that experience with their kid. It might be as simple as chaperoning on a field trip to a play, but it's still a way to connect.

Tip 3: What if there's no theatre at your local school? One very sad fact is that the performing arts in schools, particularly public schools in America, are often the first programs to be cut. It's quite possible that you want to engage your kids in a theatre community but don't know where to start. In this case, try searching for local community theaters in your area. Many offer classes, summer programs, or even opportunities for performances. Sometimes libraries host arts workshops. If all else fails, and your kid really wants to try, encourage them to try forming their own group with their peers. Forming an improv group takes no upfront money and is a great way to bond with a new group of kids.

Theatre is not just a technique for little kids. From the emotional regulation of the anchor technique to the fun of building bricks with your adolescent, theatre can build connections in long-lasting, meaningful ways.

Building off what we've talked in about with siblings, we next move to the differences when using these techniques in groups.

TWO'S COMPANY, THREE'S A CROWD

As a theatre practitioner, the benefits of participating in theatrical productions are obvious—from cast bonding to marveling at the finished product, from taking risks to building confidence. As a teacher, I discovered the benefits of theatre beyond its art form as a tool to engage students in core subjects from math to reading and everything in between. Improv in particular has the ability to create a safe space for all students. Establishing a strong group dynamic in the classroom is crucial for student success. Participating in improv games and exercises allows everyone equal footing; each student becomes a member of the ensemble. They must work together, find trust in one another, and accept and build on each other's ideas. And, as a parent, one can't help but notice the pure joy of my children as they engage in creative, imaginative play together.

—Michele Vicino-Coleman, theatre teacher, actor, director, and mother of two, from Maryland

If you're a teacher or caregiver at a daycare, chances are this is the chapter you've been waiting for. But this chapter goes beyond those kinds of groups.

Five years ago, I knew *exactly* how my life was about to change. Rachel and I were due to have our second child. We knew she'd be a girl, which might be a tiny bit different, but overall, yeah, no worries. We had a baby room painted. The crib was ready. I'd moved our old nursing chair beside it. We had piles of toys, some old, and some new. And one very, very excited young boy waiting to meet his sister.

For several weeks, to help Gavin prepare, we watched the same two episodes of *Daniel Tiger* with him. The show presents Daniel as he gets ready to

Two is very different than one. And three or more is a new game altogether.

meet his baby sister, Margaret, for the first time. The episodes are a genuinely adorable way to encourage very young kids who might not understand what's about to happen, as there's no longer going to be just one kid in their family—there's going to be two.

At the same time, Rachel and I were ready. We were by then professional diaper-changers, naptime experts, and bottle givers. We thought we knew what to expect when we were expecting, as the popular book goes, because we'd been there, done that. But we were not ready—and neither was Gavin.

While our *Daniel Tiger* intro seemed golden on the surface, Gavin was at first confused when we didn't have a baby tiger. We had a baby human. Go figure.

As for me and my wife, well, it was easier in many respects. The birth itself, the expectations around feedings, wake-ups, and so on. Yet, once again, the entire world was thrown off its axis and hurled into space. As surprised as Gavin was to encounter a baby human, we were surprised at how different everything was.

For starters, Gabby didn't like me. It sounds like a joke or an overgeneralization, but it's true. I was the primary caregiver as a stay-at-home dad, and she wouldn't let me near her. Rachel and I joked that maybe the hospital had mistakenly left the umbilical cord attached.

Things progressed and, of course, Gabby and I developed our own bond in time—though it did take some serious brick building on both our parts. The next challenge was a shift in the dynamics. Playtime wasn't one-on-one anymore. Now there were two. Both wanted all the attention, and neither wanted to share. Which brings us to the crux of this chapter:

Two is very different than one. And three or more is a new game altogether.

We were wrong. We did not know what to expect when we were expecting. We might as well have asked for a baby tiger!

. . . . .

When teaching actual improv, there's often a gap between two person scenes and larger scenes. The rules and guidelines are all the same, but the dynamics are completely different. Let's take a look at the very same rules, and then I'll show you how to apply them.

1. Say *yes, and.*
2. Say *no, but.*
3. Keep adding.
4. Avoid questions.
5. Don't break the bricks.
6. Stay in the moment.
7. Be specific.
8. Toys are not necessarily your friends.
9. Don't plan ahead!
10. Go big!
11. Always carry your anchor.

First ***yes, and.***

This core rule of all improv is honestly harder to do when there are more people interacting at once. If you're looking to have an intense, Making It Up session with two or more kids, it's going to feel different.

Every brick is valid. And ideally, everyone accepts every brick.

In true improv theatre, this is the skill that led to my improv team creating a single ninety-minute story with subplots. It's the skill that lets full-length improvisation performances dazzle audiences—even fully improvised musicals.

Yet, just as we mentioned your role as guide, the greater the number of kids at once, the greater the odds that you're going to see some major brick smashing. It's quite natural for some children to start asserting their bricks loudly over others. If you've ever seen playtime like this, you know it's a bit like watching *Lord of the Flies* or a documentary on survival of the fittest. Whichever kid is the bossiest or loudest (or both) usually insists on getting their way, until everyone else complies.

Well, that type of play is not going to end well.

Luckily, you are there as guide. Your role is essential. Watch for bricks, and make sure they're being accepted. Also watch for even distribution. If one kid is pitching every idea, the others are not being heard. And guess what? Whether you are at home with a growing family, leading a group of twenty at summer camp, or presenting at a leadership seminar, these same rules still apply.

How does this work?

While questions are often things to be avoided, try using questions to redirect bricks. For example, let's look at brothers John, age eight, and Tyler, age six. They're both playing with their mom, Betty. John's used to getting his way. He is a bit louder and more assertive than his little brother. Tyler loves playing with John, but often doesn't know what to say, so usually he lets John take the lead. Note that twenty minutes before this, the boys asked Mom to play, but she was busy. She told them she'd play once she could (rule two: *no, but*). Now let's see the play in action.

John: We're dino-robots. [Crouches and holds arms in T-rex-like pose.]

Betty: [Crouches in a similar manner.] Beep, beep. We will be late for dino robot school. Mom will be mad at us kids.

(*Betty accepted John's brick and added to it. Now they are all kids, and are late to school.*)

John: Beep, beep, Roooooaaar. I'm never going to school! I will destroy this forest!

Betty: Beep, roar. Beep, roar.

Tyler: [Joins in, acts like a robot.]

Betty: [Moving slower.] I am slowing . . . need oil. Help, I am rusting . . .

John: [Rushes over.] Oil, oil. All better! Roar!

(*At this point, Betty is concerned that Tyler hasn't added a single brick. He's following and playing, but not engaged as an equal. While Betty has added a little, John continues to set the pace and energy for all three. This is not sustainable. So, she tries to engage Tyler directly.*)

Betty: [Looking at Tyler.] Look, here comes the robot doctor. My joints still hurt.

John: No, I fixed you, and—

Betty: [Still to Tyler.] Dr. Stegosaurus, please fix this arm. [Holds out arm.]

Tyler: [Glances at John before fixing.] Needs glue.

This is just a snippet, but it's quite common. In group dynamics, one person will naturally take the lead. Really, it's not very different from group dynamics for adults. How many meetings have you attended where one person grabs the reins, and one person says nothing? And how much stronger would the meeting have been if everyone added bricks equally?

The key, as guide, is to ensure the *yes, and* is happening and being distributed evenly. Accept bricks from all. Otherwise, someone won't be saying *yes, and* at all.

As you keep accepting bricks, make sure **everyone keeps adding bricks** (rule three above). Those bricks need to come from all sides, and if they're not, it's your job to pivot the play until they do. Both my kids know how to be overly bossy and assertive. Luckily, that often balances out, but not always.

Here's another brief example, this time with two young girls, Susan and Donna, who want to play with their dad, Barry. Both girls come into playtime with some plans.

Susan: Welcome to my nail salon.

Donna: It's my restaurant.

Barry: [Big smile.] I can't believe they opened this nail salon and restaurant combo. I'm excited.

Susan: What color nails?

Donna: The special is a hamburger.

Barry: Pink nails, and a hamburger. I need to know how everything is before I ask my true love to join me.

Susan: You mean Mommy?

Barry: I do not know her name. Not yet, but you can help me.

Barry does a fantastic job of pivoting the play before a confrontation. Both girls threw a brick in, but neither was ready to accept the other's bricks. So, Barry found a way to accept both and move forward. Susan's using nonstop questions and not adding quite as much, but she's engaged and joining in with the others. The group dynamic is balanced.

As you go through the rest of the rules, it all comes down to balance. **Avoiding questions** (rule four), especially as guide, can really help the bricks continue to build. Susan will soon start mirroring her dad, and adding as the balanced scene progresses.

This brings us to rule five. **Don't break the bricks.**

Part of your role as the guide is to monitor brick breaking. In a two-person playtime, you're hopefully at the point where there's no brick breaking at all. Those are the best play sessions of all. In a group playtime, especially if it's one of your first times trying these techniques, there will almost definitely be brick breaking. Again, to compare to the office meeting for adults, at some point, someone's ideas are going to get shut down or bulldozed over. Hopefully not your ideas, but I suspect you know how it feels when that happens.

Brick breaking is tough to remedy in the moment, unless you essentially ignore the breaking. Look back at Barry in the above example. Donna broke her sister's brick, but Barry pivoted, finding a way that both bricks could work together. This type of guiding and nudging will take practice. Some of these sessions might go wrong, but keep trying and reminding yourself of the rules you're aiming for.

The next few rules are all essentially the same in group dynamics. **Stay in the moment** and **be specific** (rules six and seven) are pretty simple. You want to keep the improv moving, so you focus on what's happening around you. You keep your bricks as specific and narrow as possible. A rocket to Mars is more specific than a vehicle. A one-legged dog from the pound is a better brick than an animal.

Rules eight, nine, and ten (**toys, don't plan ahead**, and **go big**) are all identical to playtime with one. There's just another person now—or a few other people. Note that structured games are not improv-based. They can still be super fun, but if you're playing Monopoly, for instance, you're focused on the rules of that game. You aren't necessarily using your imagination or building on your own creativity. Structured games, from card games to board games, can be wonderful. Yet, the Making It Up Method is an entirely different type of connection. The amount of listening, attention, and focus required helps build a deeper bond than you'd use in a purchased game.

If you're in a classroom, the dynamic is obviously different from the dynamic you'd find at home. From day one, you've established rules, procedures, and structures. You, as the teacher, are the leader. But with improv, you are an equal. This is why this type of group play can be so empowering to young kids. Acting as their equal, just for a few minutes, is a fun way to encourage creativity while showing them new ways to interact. I know there are time constraints and curricula to follow, so try incorporating a bit of improv play into a lesson. For instance, if you're studying the water cycle, have the kids act it out. Perhaps one group of children begins as molecules in the ocean, then start moving quicker until they "evaporate" into the clouds. What types of body movements can they show to help explain their shift, especially as they "rain" later in the cycle? This type of play isn't as organic as a free intense play session, but it's still going to follow all the principles and still teach kids in a fun and meaningful manner. My favorite improv-based activity as a teacher was one I used to teach European medieval theatre. All the kids engaged in play-acting the emergence of knights, the Catholic Church, and the formation of plays on wagons as a means to communicate to crowds.

Find an activity you want to teach and try adding some improv into the mix. For example, if you're reading a book as a class, host a mock interview of the characters. This is a fantastic way to assess comprehension while the kids still get to improvise, pretending to be the characters from the book. Another example could come if you're studying science. Can the students improvise inertia? What would it look like if one kid just kept going unless another force acted upon them? Can you play-act as gravity or momentum? Once you've introduced the topic and concept of improv, focus on the rules above. *Yes, and* in particular allows kids to build off their peers' ideas. If possible, avoid breaking bricks in the moment, and then, at the end of the playtime, go back and address any factual errors that might have crept in. This is a great skill builder in interpersonal relations and confidence for kids as well. Keep in mind these types of activities could be used in camp and conference settings as well.

We've worked down to our last rule: **always carry your anchor**. Anchors in group play are essential. This final technique will be the difference between having a fun time and having a miserable one. I can fully attest that many days as both a parent and as a teacher, I've found the anchor to be a lifesaver. The stronger the group dynamics, and the crazier the playtimes become, the more strongly I find myself clinging to my anchor.

Remember your anchor is individual to *you*. It is any memory that helps you feel optimistic. It does not need to be related to the kids you're interacting with during playtime at all. If your anchor isn't working, you need to choose a stronger one. A good anchor is an intense memory that works anywhere. You don't need a different anchor for school or home, as long as your anchor is strong enough to keep you grounded and optimistic.

I remember when I first started substitute teaching, after being a SAHD.

It was post-pandemic, and the school district had a sign-up begging adults to consider subbing. The shortages in the schools were out of control. My kids had both started at their own schools, so my days had freed. I signed up.

On one of those mornings, I was placed in a high school math room. Subbing isn't teaching, mind you. Two of the kids grabbed their phones and started filming as another started throwing things at me until I called for backup. Yeah, it takes a crazy thick skin to sub. But it also takes an anchor. In that moment, as a water bottle missed my face by mere inches, I found myself focusing on Gavin. I was doing this to earn a bit of extra money and help his school district. I was doing this for him.

It's hopefully not that crazy when you start trying some group-intense improv time. But it might be. The more people, the higher the energy. The stronger you need to be as guide, and the tougher it can feel emotionally. If the play is not going the way you'd hoped, try refocusing your energy on your anchor a moment before jumping in to guide more closely.

The more people try to do this sort of intense improv-based play at once, the more fun you can have—or the more quickly it can collapse. Let's take a look at a successful group improv-led interaction. As you read, look for all the moments of *yes, and* that the adult uses, even when the kids don't use *yes, and* at first. In this example, Brad is a teacher, and the rest are kids. Brad is leading his gym students in a mock snowball fight.

Brad: These soft cotton balls are actually snowballs.

Tilly: Brr, my hands are cold.

Brad: You're right, Tilly. They're too cold to hold. Let's all put on gloves. [Puts on imaginary gloves.]

Jake: They're not really cold.

Brad: Exactly, when touched through these gloves, they're not really so bad. Now, when I count to three, we all will throw the snowballs. One, two, three!

Emily: Look out!

Shay: Can't hit me, I have a force field.

Brad: Shay built a force field, but it only lasts five seconds.

Connor: I want a force field.

Brad: Hold your arms out to build a force field.

Jake: I don't need a force field. Take that!

Brad: Ah, he got me!

You get the idea. In the scene above, Brad didn't just give directions, he used *yes, and* as well as basic improv skills to keep the class moving forward. Jake wasn't necessarily on board, but Brad redirected while still acknowledging that he heard and accepted the comment.

This type of dynamic can take practice, or even private coaching. Every scenario is going to be different, and the application of the Making It Up Method is going to take some practice. For teachers especially, consider looking at www.christophermannino.com/improvforgroups.html for some extra resources toward group improv dynamics.

The final takeaway for this chapter is to not be afraid to involve more people. Whether it's your other children at home or a class full of kids at school, improv and theatre skills can change the way everyone interacts. And if you give it some practice, it can be an awful lot of fun.

It won't be perfect. But in the next chapter, you'll learn how you can get better and better at making it up!

BETTER

The concept of *yes, and* is one that I'm incredibly familiar with as someone who has done improv for more the last thirty-three years of my life. Implementing this simple tool into play with my two children, ages three and two, is insanely valuable as it allows their minds to run and go anywhere their hearts desire. Seeing the imagination spark as I continued down the path of *yes, and* with them and seeing the journey we'd take with our play was so heartwarming and often led to us laughing so much with the nonsense they'd piece together. The more I do improv, the better I get at the skills. Every time you say *yes, and*, it gets easier to accept and add bricks. I can't recommend this enough—a simple but valuable tool to have in one's parenting bag that leads to imaginative play. Well done!

—Peter Allwine, direct service provider and father of two, from South Dakota

I'm a perfectionist. In most aspects of my life, I prefer to be in total control and have everything turn out amazing. The problem is, that's not how life works. And it's especially not how parenting works.

There is no perfect parent.

I'm going to say that again, for those in the back seats.

THERE IS *NO* PERFECT PARENT.

Do you remember when you were waiting for your first child to be born, and you went through the rigorous four-year training program, with a certificate of "Perfect Parent" presented at the end? No? Me neither. And it's not just parenting. Improv, by its nature, is unpredictable. I have plenty of examples, but your playtimes will be different. What's more, if you're following this book closely, every single playtime will be different than the one before it!

There's a lot to be said for familiarity. It's why people watch shows, or play video games, or read books in a series. As a fantasy writer, I find myself going back to repeat characters for the same reason. It's why families will take out the deck of playing cards, or the board game everyone likes. It's a sense of comfort. Of knowing what to expect.

In improv, there's no expectation.

DON'T PLAN AHEAD!

This rule is essential, but it's also frustrating to many parents. How can your playtimes be perfect when you've no idea what's going to happen? How do you know that today's playtime won't be a total disaster? How do you know that trying something fun and exciting while out of the house won't embarrass you all?

Simply, you don't.

You don't know what will happen. And you have no idea if it will be great, or even good. But you try anyway. Every day. Ten minutes a day. And as you clutch your anchor, I want you to do something else. Let go of the idea of perfect. As I said, it doesn't exist.

Let's break it down into some realistic chunks.

Accept That You Will Make Mistakes.

You're human. If you're not, then you shouldn't be reading this.[1] And being human means you make mistakes. I am certainly no exception.

I've shared a number of examples already of personal failures. From throwing a temper tantrum in front of Gavin to falling apart due to my own overeagerness to do everything on the first day of lockdown. There are plenty of others.

My family was visiting Hershey, Pennsylvania. We have ties to the area and go frequently. It's quite a sweet place, if you'll pardon the pun. This, however, was our first time with the kids. And we wanted to show them everything.

I was the one who strongly suggested the Indian Echo Caverns. It's a limestone cave we'd visited before. Lovely stalactites and stalagmites. I thought Gavin might really enjoy it, as the kids had never gone caving.

The cavern is accessible only by guided tour, and each tour lasts about forty-five minutes. Gabby had been having a rough trip already. In fact, our first night at the Hershey Lodge, she and I wandered the empty hallways because she couldn't sleep. The staff kept offering extra Hershey bars and even made me coffee from the staff room, but it was still tough. You'd think that sort of trip would give us pause before diving below the surface of the earth. Well, we took the plunge.

After three minutes, Gabby's mouth opened about ten sizes wider than her height (yes, it's that horror movie trope, but you get the image). Then the screams began. If you were on the East Coast, particularly the Mid-Atlantic, I'm pretty sure you heard them in the distance. The entire cavern trembled and shook under the ferocity of that tantrum. And it lasted forty minutes. The guide wouldn't help us. The people on the tour looked at us as if we'd ruined their day. And Gabby wouldn't let me console her, demanding that Rachel carry her every torturous step.

When we emerged, I felt like an utter failure. I'd literally dragged her to Hell. And I hadn't just failed Gabby. I'd failed Rachel, by insisting we go and making an already tough trip far harder. I'd failed Gavin by ensuring his first trip to a cave was a miserable memory. I just felt horrible.

We left the trip early. As we were driving back, Rachel and I were consumed by a sense of defeat. We said we'd probably give up trying to bring the kids anywhere at all. (Our next trip would end up being amazing, just a few months later.) As we drove, and the storm settled around us, I reached for my anchor.

There'd been a moment during the trip where both Gavin and Gabby sipped giant milkshakes. That was my anchor then.

KEEP MOVING FORWARD

There have been countless other moments where I felt like I did poorly. Countless moments of failure or disappointment. I've lost my temper, I've cried, I've made mistakes. The anchor helps, but it is equally important to keep moving forward. You might stumble, but you still get back up. There's a lovely moment in the film *Inside Out 2* where Joy breaks down. She is a literal representation of happiness and optimism, but when confronted by an anxiety attack, she yells, cries, and loses her temper. And then, she wipes her tears and keeps going, essentially grabbing her anchor again. Moving forward is key.

YOUR KIDS ARE NOT YOU

This is a broad one, but it matters a lot. Many parents feel like a failure if their kid does something wrong, or if the kid fails at something. This is simply a logical fallacy. If the kid can't ride a bike the first time they try, are they a bike failure? If they're not potty trained the first time you point to a toilet, are they a potty failure? No, obviously not.

In a similar vein, if your kid has a loud tantrum, it's not a reflection on you. Even if that tantrum's in the middle of a plane or the middle of a long, dark cavern tour. You'll get nasty looks. Rude people might even complain. You know what? Let them. It's not your fault. And you're doing everything you can. I've been blessed with kids who fly well. But I've seen others who don't. And it's a weird environment. Pressure building in your ears, seats crammed with uncomfortable strangers. And a window showing you thousands of feet above the world. It's weird! If your kid cries because of all that, it is not your fault. It's not about you. It's about them. And if any other person tries to give you grief, that's their problem not yours.

TIGHTEN THE ANCHOR

Just remembering you have an anchor isn't enough. At times, the rope binding that anchor to your heart will tense and stretch. It'll be hard to focus on the good moment, because at some point you're going to get angry or frustrated with your kids. Yes, you will. It's human nature. They are not you, and they will make their own choices. At some point, they will make a bad choice. This is normal. This is expected. And this can sometimes lead you to crawl mentally into that happy place, to remind yourself of the positivity that you might be forgetting in the moment.

A strong anchor, based on your kids, won't just help your emotional regulation; it can honestly help that relationship. It's a nice reminder of what really matters. I use this tightening the anchor technique any time the kids get me mad, and yes—they do get me mad. It's okay to get mad at your kids. Or to be sad, or frustrated, or any other emotion you feel. The emotions aren't wrong. Yet, you can manage them.

DO BETTER NEXT TIME

This is the final step of the process here. Once you recognize that you can't accept personal blame for everything your kids do, you then tighten the anchor. After this, recognize that perhaps you made mistakes. If you're feeling imperfect, *be* imperfect! We are imperfect creatures. The quality that should define us most is the power to learn from our mistakes and constantly improve. *Do better next time*. This goes for playtime, parenting, and life. It's as old as human civilization itself. If at first you don't succeed, try again.

It's such simplistic, seemingly obvious advice. Yet, for many, this third step is the hardest. I'll admit, before this method, I struggled with hyper-perfectionism. To return to that moment at the cave, I'd struggle to move forward. I'd start blaming myself and analyzing my mistake, going around in mental circles like a washing machine on infinite rinse and repeat. The trouble is that while it seems like you're just hurting yourself or punishing yourself for some mistake, you're truly hurting everyone else—especially the kids. If you wallow in self-pity, the kids won't move forward. The anchor collapses. And you won't do better next time.

As Elsa so wisely sings: "Let it go." And move forward.

o5

1. KEEP MOVING FORWARD.
2. YOUR KIDS ARE NOT YOU.
3. TIGHTEN THE ANCHOR.
4. DO BETTER NEXT TIME

There's one final element to doing better.

What Makes You a Great Parent?

I want you to pause and spend a minute thinking about what makes a parent *great*. Jot down notes if you want, but at least brainstorm a few ideas. What kind of parenting meets the definition of great in your mind? Jot down at least three ideas:

1. ____

2. ____

3. ____

Next, spend a moment thinking about where you were before reading the book. Where are you now? Are you doing *better* than before? Are you moving in the direction you hope to? Write three ways that you have personally improved as a parent, in your opinion, just since starting the book.

1. ____

2. ____

3. ____

As you think about direction and definitions, I'd like to acknowledge that most of the "rules" and expectations we hold ourselves to are completely invented. There's no one definition of great parenting. And whether you're moving in the right direction (hopefully you are) is an intensely personal question.

While writing this book, I was reading *The Code of the Extraordinary Mind* by Vishen Lakhiani. This self-help book continuously asks the reader to examine the rules that they've subconsciously set for themselves. Lakiani goes so far as to call these "bulls--- rules, or *brules*."[2] As I wrote, I started thinking about how many brules I'd adapted for my own parenting, and how every parent out there likely has their own. There's no one way to be a parent, and no one way to be great parent.

Some rules that I no longer believe:

- If a kid cries in public, you're not a good parent.
- Parents should never ask for breaks (see next chapter!).
- Stay-at-home parents don't need other adults.

I asked some of my friends and they had their own brules that they no longer like. Here are some of the top ones they suggested:

- Parents always need to be in control of every situation.
- Parents need to give constant instructions all the time.
- Kids should never question their parents.
- Every second of a kid's day should be scheduled (nonstop clubs and outings).
- Parents need to put their kids' needs first and neglect their own.

There's no perfect, only better.

NONE OF THE ABOVE ARE TRUE!

Hopefully, you're starting to see how silly some of these expectations really are.

As you go back over those notes you just took, compare to some of the brules above. There's no right or wrong way to be a parent. If a rule isn't working, change it. If you're not the kind of great parent you want to be, don't worry too much about being perfect or great; just do *better*.

There's always room to improve. If you're struggling, just focus on a few ways you can do better. If ten minutes a day without interruptions has helped, maybe one day a month of a whole-day special adventure with your kid would make a difference. If playing in your backyard was meaningful, try playing in the grocery store next time. Keep moving toward better.

The very notion of moving toward being great is a process of saying *yes, and* to your own ideas. Travel with the kid would be fun. *Yes, and* a few years of travelling the world would be even better. Sounds impossible, but it's not. My wife and I are saying *yes, and* to every possible idea. Yours don't have to be as extreme, but try saying *yes, and*, and continue to do better. There's no perfect, only better.

Helping with homework is good. Volunteering to chaperone is better. Helping with an after-school club might be even better. Keep saying *yes, and*. Keep challenging those brules that say you can't do more. The more you do, the stronger your relationships will become.

- Do better.
- Go big.
- Say *yes, and* to your own gut.

ESCAPE

As a mom who frequently used to engage in imaginative play with my oldest, I admit that the age gap between my children slowed those precious moments. I was often too tired or too busy. After reading Mannino's *yes, and* advice, I became more intentional. In just a few minutes, my seven-year-old and I went from inventing a telephone to creating a hovercraft and traveling around the world in seconds. That only took fifteen minutes of my time, and he was so happy. He was too used to "too busy" or "too tired" excuses where I would agree to watch a show or play a card game, etc., and yet it made all the difference.

—Jamie Barber, marketing manager, author of *Finney and the Secret Tunnel*, and mother of three, from Virginia

Jamie's refrain is a familiar one. How many of us often feel too tired and too busy? How many moments has exhaustion stolen from our ability to concentrate on our kids? Self-care is no joke. The anchor technique can help, but it's not enough. You also need to get away. In a parenting book, why add a chapter about getting away from the kids?

Well, for many, it's not an obvious form of self-care. Or some parents feel guilty about leaving the kids.

I remember the first evening date Rachel and I took together after we had a kid. We went to a speakeasy-style bar in town and ordered fancy grown-up drinks. Then we stared at each other, trying to stay awake. It took us a total of ten minutes before we started wondering if the kids were okay. And then the conversation started circling around how tired we were and back to the kids again.

There's a scene in the first season of *Bluey* that is so true to life, it always makes me smile. The parents, Bandit and Chilli, pretend to go on a date at a fancy restaurant, and both parents admit they don't remember what romance

Taking breaks is the true secret to parenting.

means. They also talk about how hard it can be to keep up with romance when you're constantly tired.

And the constant exhaustion is real.

My kids are wonderful. Yet they're nonstop energy. They also both have sleep issues—massive sleep issues. We had to hire a professional sleep consultant more than once. For months, I'd drive Gavin in the car for an hour just to lull him to sleep. When kids don't sleep, parents don't sleep. Perhaps you've had periods where you get a few hours each night before another kid is up complaining about the shape of the moon, the texture of their wall, or the true meaning of *Pokemon.*[1] Sleep . . . sleep is elusive at times. The chapter on faking energy comes from the heart, because I fake it a lot.

Yet, my wife and I also discovered the true secret to parenting: *taking breaks.*

It's not wrong. And it really changes everything.

Think of it this way. You buy a brand new fancy phone. You have all the latest apps and love using it for both work and play. However, you decide that because the phone is meant to be on, you're never going to charge it. How long is that phone going to last?

EVERY DEVICE IN OUR TECH-RIDDLED WORLD NEEDS CHARGING. AND SO DO WE.

Sleep is important. Find a routine and sneak in naps. Hire a consultant if you need to.

Yet there's the other form of recharge which is just as critical: *escape.*

You Also Need to Recharge

Take a break. Find a babysitter. Or ask a family member to watch the kids. Plan a night out. There's a new suggested rule circulating called the *2-2-2 rule*. The idea is to go on a date every two weeks, a weekend getaway every two months, and a weeklong vacation every two years. This idea, originally posted on Reddit, has even been discussed on the Familius blog as a great way to grow your adult relationships.

Unfortunately, this won't work for all parents. My wife and I have had kids for nearly eight years and have never been away from the kids overnight. We

simply don't have a sitter or family member willing to watch them at this point. Forget the weeklong trips, we can't even envision a weekend getaway. And I know for many other parents of young kids, the 2-2-2 rule sounds more like a fantasy. How, then, can you ensure that you're getting breaks and building your relationship?

First, make sure you plan regular dates. Rachel and I try to schedule three date days a month. These are days where we can escape, take a break from the kids, and reconnect with each other. Budgeting both time and cost for these sitter days is not optional, it's a top priority for our family. And once we moved to this method, our stress decreased, our joy increased, and the relationship we had with the kids grew as well. Make sure you schedule regular date days with your spouse. If you're a single parent, schedule time with friends or even with yourself.

YOU NEED SPACE TO BE AN ADULT.

Second, mix up those date ideas. If every date is dinner and a movie, you're going to be boring yourselves pretty fast. The internet is your friend. Find the

Find ways to build—add your relationship bricks.

new! Go check out a new park, a museum, a winery. Go see a play or try a karaoke night or visit a place you've never been. Variety is key. For some, a skill that helps is remembering to say *yes, and*. You're going to look at some ideas of events around you and feel unsure. Is that something you'd enjoy? Worth the drive or the cost?

Yes, and can be a powerful motivator to trying new things on dates and for building connections. In a similar vein, constantly find ways to build—add your relationship bricks. It doesn't matter if you've been together one year or one hundred, there's always more to discuss and discover.

And . . . if you want to really try these skills while building the relationship with your spouse and maintaining your time as an adult, why not try an improv workshop or show? Now's the perfect opportunity!

I'd like to encourage the creation of two very different, but equally important things: a Journal of Me and a Journal of Us.

The Journal of ME

This is what it sounds like. A personal journal for you to reflect on yourself. If you keep a diary or scrapbook, feel free to borrow a few pages there. Your children are building their unique identities; it's time to revisit your identity. I've seen countless parents, especially stay-at-home parents, who get so immersed in being Mom or Dad that they cease to recognize themselves beyond that. On a playdate with a friend, a mother admitted to me that she'd signed up for a local choir solely to be in a place where no one called her Mommy.

In your journal, make sure you highlight five things that you enjoy. Not things your kids enjoy, but things you enjoy yourself. If it helps, write them now. Quick, go grab that journal.

Now, write down five new things you'd like to try. Something you've never done. Perhaps a photography course or learning to ski. Anything at all. Try writing five things you want to try now.

This is the beginning of your *Journal of Me*. The journal you need to use toward self-monitoring. It's important to have unique passions and interests. It's okay if they overlap with your kids'. Yet, find something to be excited about on your own as well. Keep in mind, watching TV isn't an active thing to add to this list. Focus on new things you genuinely want to try. And as crazy as it might sound to try something new at your age, this is the *perfect* time to start.

Yes, and get to it.

PUT A RECURRING REMINDER ON YOUR PHONE. RIGHT NOW.
SET THE REMINDER ON YOUR CALENDAR.
THE REMINDER IS SIMPLY "SELF-CHECK."

Whenever that pops up, open to your lists. Are you making time for the activities you enjoy? Are you trying some of the new things? Maybe there's something else you want to add to that list? Once a month, do a personal self-care check. You can't build relationships if you're not taking care of yourself.

The Journal of US

This list is specific for any parent who has a spouse or significant other adult relationship in their life. The "US" is you and your partner. While you're building bonds with your kids and maintaining your relationship with your own mental health, you also need to focus on the two of you.

This is building off the chapter's opening. Get away. Escape. And spend time together.

Want a major secret? It's okay to schedule sex. If life's too busy and too hectic, then go and add it to the calendar. It might sound unromantic, but better to add it now than neglect it entirely.

Similar to the previous journal, I want you to think about five things you enjoy doing with your partner. I want you to write those five, and note the frequency that you are doing them. For this activity, don't just list bedroom activities. Maybe it's holding hands on a walk with just the two of you or a conversation at a coffee shop. Maybe it's a massage or a museum visit. For each item below, I want you to write how many times you've done this activity with your partner over the past three months. Try a chart like this:

ACTIVITY YOU ENJOY WITH YOUR PARTNER	HOW OFTEN IN LAST 3 MONTHS?
1.	
2.	
3.	
4.	
5.	

This is a great place to start. As mentioned earlier, try to start scheduling regular dates together. It is okay to ask for babysitting help. As you start working on enjoying some of the above more often, make a second list together:

SOMETHING NEW TO TRY	SCHEDULE IT
1.	
2.	
3.	
4.	
5.	

The key to the table above is that you're not just thinking of new and fun ideas, you're *scheduling* them: "We should try this." "*Yes, and*—it's on the calendar!"

Beyond just going out together, make sure you and your significant other are creating anchor-style memories together. These memories, in turn, will help strengthen your emotional resilience when you're bond-building with your kids. It all comes full circle. The time you're putting in for yourself and your partner will be rewarded triple-fold when you go to play and interact with your kids. Remember, kids are sponges, and they will see your strength and want to mirror it themselves.

Remember, kids are sponges, and they will see your strength and want to mirror it themselves.

There's more from this book to take with you during those moments with yourself and your partner. The theatre skills you've focused on up until now all center around *listening*, *observing*, and *building*. Every time you've joined an improv, you've listened to bricks and observed ideas so you can add and stay in the moment. Every time you've used an anchor, you've focused your emotional energy on positivity. These skills can help with self-reflection and growth. And they can be especially helpful when continuing to build a relationship with your partner.

LISTEN, OBSERVE, BUILD, AND PUT YOUR ENERGY TOWARD THE POSITIVE.

Your relationships will soar to new heights.

SHOWTIME

I noticed my daughter was tired and about to have a meltdown, so I decided to try Chris's method and initiated imaginative play. It was such a pleasant surprise (and huge relief for both of us) that we moved through an almost-meltdown into a state of laughter and joy. This book is a wonderful reminder to put down our phones and take the time to connect with our children! There is always room for a stronger bond, no matter how close you already are!

—Caroline Gilman, business owner and mother of one, from California

TAKE A BOW!

You've made it through the techniques to the big finale. I'm going to sum up everything you've learned, and give some examples. Remember, just as Caroline discovered, there's always room for a stronger bond, and now you have the tools to build one. The spotlight is on you moving forward. And remember any time you feel that you need a bit more coaching or support, head on over to www.ChristopherMannino.com/MIU for tons of extras.

By now, I hope you've had some of the most amazing playtimes ever. And those are just the beginning. Keep building, keep playing, keep forming anchor memories! The more often you use these skills, the more they'll make a genuine difference in your life. If you're doing this right, you should be having *fun*. You should be enjoying every minute of this type of play. You should be feeling better and better about yourself, your kids, and your relationships.

Making It Up Method vs. Parent-Child Interaction Therapy

To contrast, I mentioned that my wife and I used Parent-Child Interaction Therapy (PCIT) for a time. This is a well-proven, psychology-based, scripted therapy approach. It involves a psychiatrist monitoring how you play with your kids and essentially telling you everything you do is wrong, unless you are following the exact script of when and what to say and do, right down to giving time-outs with a script.

I tried. I really wanted to believe in PCIT. And I'm sure it works for many. But I ended up stopping one of our sessions in the middle (this was via Zoom) and just saying "I'm done." Then I logged off.

Why?

Because everything about that technique made me feel bad. I felt like I hated myself as a parent. I hated spending the scripted, forced time with my kids. Every forced command and punishment I gave felt wrong in every fiber of my being. And throughout the entire process, I realized that joy had been completely sapped from my playtime. The PCIT daily playtime wasn't just work, it was a chore—even a stress.

In many ways, the techniques I advocate in this book are a response to what we went through. I understand there's a ton of research out there backing how effective PCIT can be. Maybe that method worked for your family, or was necessary. Still, I believe parenting should be fun. It should be something that brings people together naturally and makes all involved feel stronger and better about themselves.

After I logged out of that PCIT session, feeling angry and tense, I spent thirty minutes of intense unscripted, naturally improvised time with Gabby. Those thirty minutes were more meaningful and more positive than anything we'd done in the three months prior with PCIT.

DO WHAT WORKS FOR YOU.
DO WHAT FEELS RIGHT FOR YOUR FAMILY.
AND LET PARENTING BE FUN.

. . . . .

So, in keeping it fun . . .

Let's sum up the basics.

First, the core ideas:

1. Say *yes, and.*
2. Say *no, but.*
3. Keep adding.
4. Avoid questions.
5. Don't break the bricks.
6. Stay in the moment.
7. Be specific.
8. Toys are not necessarily your friends.
9. Don't plan ahead!
10. Go big!
11. Always carry your anchor.

Have you noticed that the bulk of the time was spent on *yes, and* and anchors? These are the bookends, the pillar ideas that hold everything else up.

The Two Pillars

By now, you understand that saying *yes, and* to ideas is a fundamental way to listen, connect, and build during playtime. Those simple words are revolutionary and are hopefully already making a big difference in the way you interact with kids.

Yes, and isn't just an idea or technique. It means listening, observing, accepting, affirming, and building. This progression will change playtime, relationships, and life in general. It is the core to a growing, thriving relationship between you and your kids.

The anchor is your second pillar. While rooted in method acting, the anchor technique is a form of emotional regulation that, if used correctly, will change everything. When I first presented a talk about the anchor technique, I wasn't certain how it would be received. Weeks later, people I didn't know continued to approach me, telling me I'd changed their lives. The anchor allows you to refocus your attention on positivity.

***Yes, and* isn't just an idea or technique. It means listening, observing, accepting, affirming, and building.**

In essence, it brings hope amidst the hopeless moments. That's a superpower that cannot be underestimated.

For those of you who like to go deep, the psychological basis of the anchor is called "attentional deployment." This method of emotional regulation is well documented as an effective way of dealing with emotions. By focusing attention on positive memories, individuals can better regulate their own moods. In 2015, researchers Jamie Ferri at the University of California–Santa Cruz and Greg Hajcak at Stony Brook University studied the effects of attentional deployment on emotional regulation:

> Individuals can control attention to emotion by employing attentional deployment (AD), an emotion regulation (ER) strategy that typically involves shifting attention away from emotional information in the service of reducing emotional impact.[1]

By placing the attention and the energy on your anchor, you're regulating your mood. In a study published in *Personality and Social Psychology Review*, Heather Wadlinger and Derek Isaacowitz maintain that "selective attention to positive information reflects emotion regulation, and that regulating attention is a critical component of the emotion regulatory process."[2] In other words, focusing attention on something positive, such as an anchor, can help people keep calm. Regulating where your attention lies is critical for keeping your emotions in balance. Think of *Inside Out 2*. All of Riley's attention is focused on Anxiety, so much so that she breaks down. It's not until she can draw her attention back to Joy that she finds the equilibrium to move forward.

The anchor itself remains rooted in Konstantin Stanislavski's method acting and skills of emotional recall. For actors reading this, throw in some of Lee Strasberg's sense memories as you focus on every detail around your anchor. The revolutionary change is that these methods aren't to help a character, they're to help you regulate your own moods. Beyond simple attentional deployment, the theatre skills tap into another field of psychology called *temporal distancing*. By allowing yourself to live in another, more positive time, you can more easily access the emotions and calming power of your anchor in the present. While temporal distancing is often focused on envisioning a positive future, it can also be used to strongly recall a positive past. The difference cognitively between past and future is actually zero.[3] Pair this with the growing studies in temporal distancing, where subjects are asked to envision a strong, positive future to change their mood. A 2022 study in San Fransico, for instance, found that frequent use of temporal distancing greatly lowered stress.[4]

Anchors work. There is science to back them up. And they're a remarkably easy and accessible way to change your life.

Yes, that's a lot of technical talk, but the point remains: anchors work. There is science to back them up. And they're a remarkably easy and accessible way to change your life.

The anchor and the *yes, and* improv skill are the two pillars of the Making It Up Method. Between those two pillars are the skills and tips you've seen throughout the book. The small tweaks and changes that make the difference between good playtime and great playtime.

In fact, kids know a lot about theatre already. Kids are naturals at improvisation and play-acting. From a very young age, imaginative play is instinctual. Yet, where you've been this entire time is a zone of development that encourages both you and the kids to go much, much further. This is a zone I first learned about from my college mentor Rosalind Flynn.

> **Mannino's advice and guidance for play-based parenting is a natural extension of educational psychologist Lev Vygotsky's key construct called the Zone of Proximal Development (ZPD). The ZPD is that space between what children can do alone and how much more they can do in collaboration with adults. Try play-based parenting activities and watch a child's imagination, vocabulary, and problem-solving abilities expand!**
>
> **—Dr. Rosalind Flynn, Catholic University**

Yep, while I didn't specify before, this entire book centers you as a guide to push through the ZPD and bring your children to amazing new places. Just remember, the book isn't meant to be read or listened to. It's meant to be *practiced*. The more you try, the more you'll get out of it.

Let's take a look at two final, longer examples of Making It Up in action. In the first, I'll point out some of what's happening. In the second, use what you've learned to break it down on your own.

Scenario One

John is a dad, playing with his son, Connor, age five.

> **Connor: Welcome to the zoo!**
>
> **(*Brick: location.*)**
>
> **John: Thanks, Mr. Smith. I'm excited to interview for the new job. I've always wanted to be a zookeeper.**
>
> **(Yes, and. *Be specific. Three bricks added.*)**
>
> **Connor: Oh, I'm sorry, the zookeeper job is now closed. You will interview to be the new penguin.**
>
> ***(This is not smashing a brick—he accepted his role as Mr. Smith, he accepted that John wanted to be a zookeeper, and he accepted that John was there to interview. He then added a new brick: the surprise new job.)***

John: [Scratching his arms like an ape while grinning.] I didn't know gorillas could be penguins

(Yes, and *continues, and added a brick about himself, also avoided questions.*)

Connor: You might be the first. We can only afford to pay in bananas. (*Yes, and.*)

John: I love bananas!

(*Yes, and.*)

Connor: Me too. Come sit down, Hank the gorilla. I'm very impressed with your resume.

(*Avoids using toys, and mimes looking at a paper.*)

John: It took me a while to learn to write in chalk. I used to only use poop.

(*Specific, stay in moment.*)

Connor: Well, it's a good thing you learned, you're perfect. Follow me.

(*As John follows Connor through the make-believe zoo, he's reminded of his own struggles to find a new job. He thinks briefly about a recent interview that went totally wrong. As the storm threatens to interrupt playtime, he focuses his attention on his anchor—a memory of his anniversary dinner with his wife last week. This anchor memory builds in strength and he clings to it, bringing his mind back to a place of positivity.*)

Connor: You'll need to wear this suit.

(*Brick.*)

John: [Puts on imaginary suit.] Ugh, this smells like fish.

(*Brick.*)

Connor: No it doesn't. Wear this hat too.

(*Connor broke John's brick, but John remains the guide.*)

John: I like this hat. Oooh my stomach's growling, I hope penguins eat bananas.

(*Brick, avoided questions.*)

Connor: [Falls to ground.] Look out, it's the flying crocodile gang!

(*Specific, adding, going big.*)

John: I see them. I'm throwing my ninja hat! [Jumps in the air.]

(*He's really grateful for the anchor, which is in full power now, as he's refocused on the playtime. He also has an idea about the earlier broken brick.*)

Connor: They dodge and have fire swords!

(*Staying in present, brick.*)

John: I thought I smelled fish! Come on other penguins, toss your fish over the fence like this. Look, the croc gang is going after the fish, we're saved!

(Yes, and, *keep adding, going big, specific, bringing back a broken brick.*)

Connor: And you are hired!

John: Ooh, ooh, I'm such a happy gorilla! I'm gonna call my mom!

The above scene could keep going, but hopefully it helped to break down the bricks, rules, and even the moment when John tapped into his anchor. Here's one more scenario of strong play. This time, see if you can spot all the techniques on your own.

Scenario Two

Maria is Ashley's mom. Ashley is five.

Ashley: Welcome to my salon!

Maria: Happy to be here, I'd like a mani-pedi.

Ashley: But you're a robot.

Maria: A robot who loves mani-pedis. I have to look good for my date.

Ashley: Oh, tell me about your date. Another robot?

Maria: Oh no, she's an astronaut. That's why I want my nails all done green. It's her favorite color. Beep. Beep.

Ashley: Wow, I love astronauts.

Maria: Me too! Beep. Beep. And pizza! That pizza on the counter smells delicious.

Ashley: It's anchovies and boiled rabbit.

Maria: My favorite flavors! And Sheila's too. That's her name.

Ashley: Wait, I know Sheila! The astronaut who discovered aliens on the moon.

Maria: Yes, she is popular. She built me when the aliens made her mad. Beep beep. Call incoming. Buzzzzzzz. Oh no, Sheila has canceled our date. She has married an alien instead.

Ashley: I'm sorry, here, have a slice of pizza.

Maria: My heart program is increasing. Perhaps you will go on a date with me tonight? We are going bowling.

Ashley: Only if you do my mani-pedi next. I like green too!

How'd you do? Did you notice the rules being followed?

The intense play you've been doing throughout this book is only the beginning. Yet, I want to emphasize again that it should feel good and fun. Trust your gut. There is no perfect parent. There is no perfect parenting technique, either. Yet, if done correctly, the Making It Up Method can bring new levels of depth and fun to your relationships.

Take a bow.

Then dive back in. And keep going.

Enjoy every second with your kids.

Especially the times when you're all *Making It Up*!

TOOL KIT: YOUR BRICKYARD

As I read, I couldn't help but think about an experience we had at the dinner table not too long ago. My four-and-a-half-year-old, John, is a very picky eater, and we have a hard time getting him to eat enough protein. One night at dinner, my husband offered the first improv brick: "If you eat enough chicken to reach your toes, I bet we could smell it!"

John, always a mama's boy, turned to me, "You think so Mommy?" Next came my *yes, and*...

> "Oh definitely, your feet might even start to squawk like a chicken."
>
> Before I knew it, chicken was being consumed, feet were being sniffed, and loud clucking surrounded our dinner table. To some it may have been chaos. To us, it was family fun at the dinner table while my child happily (and finally) consumed his protein!
>
> —Elizabeth Ferrante, theatre teacher and mother of three, from Virginia

For many, the theatre in this book is still new. Not everyone can create bricks on the fly, especially when they're just starting. While most kids are natural improvisers, adults might need a bit of extra help—whether to help their child eat their dinner or simply to play. Most importantly, remember that as you are creating or building bricks you are strengthening bonds with your child!

This final bonus chapter is your brickyard. Feel free to come here for ideas whenever you're feeling low. Or if it helps, flip through through these before your next intense play session. While it's usually best to avoid planning, a few bricks in hand can't hurt.

Relationships and Occupations

Characters begin with relationships. Is the kid you're about to play with your dad? Your pilot? Your chef? Here are some possibilities:

Father	Inventor	Student
Mother	Creation	Coach
Brother	Trash collector	Husband
Sister	Waiter	Wife
Son	Tour guide	Love interest
Daughter	Pet owner	Rival
Grandkid	Friend	Mentor
Grandparent	Stranger	Roommate
Cousin	Thief	Neighbor
Boss	Doctor	Confidant
Employee	Teacher	General

- Ally
- Director
- Stylist
- Newscaster
- Social media influencer
- Fortune teller
- Zookeeper
- Candymaker
- Clown
- Dentist
- Train engineer
- Chef
- Gardener

Where is this scene happening? There's a world of difference between a conversation in school and a conversation on Mars. Let your imagination run to new locals:

- Home
- Moon
- Under the sea
- School
- Barbershop
- Mall
- Park
- Mountain
- Beach
- Boat
- Amusement park
- Closed/abandoned amusement park
- Spaceship
- Grandma's house
- Woods
- Store
- Cemetery
- Pizza shop
- Restaurant
- Castle
- Church
- Canyon
- Zoo
- Robot factory
- Factory
- Microscopic world
- Clouds
- Airplane
- Jungle
- Desert
- Middle Earth
- Hogwarts
- Bluey's house
- Narnia
- Atlantis
- Ancient Rome

Goals

What does your character want? A strong goal can really drive playtime, because it gives you something to constantly move towards. In a similar way, throwing obstacles against these goals can be fun too. If your goal is to discover a new planet, maybe the spaceship's broken. Every goal usually has a fun obstacle to play with. Try these goals:

- Fall in love
- Money
- Power
- Friendship
- Discover a new place
- Build something
- Unclog something
- Hide something
- Return something unwanted

Hide somewhere
Travel
Get help
Fix something broken
Heal your illness
Become king or queen
Defeat the villain
Rescue the princess
Eat
Escape
Solve a case
Buy something
Find treasure
Land a job
Make the sale
Win the race
Find a new outfit
Teach
Make people laugh

Emotions and Moods

What are you feeling when the playtime starts? A happy character is going to respond very differently from an angry one. Think about your goals—how do they make you feel? Maybe one of these emotions or moods:

Happy
Sad
Angry
Jealous
Afraid
Anxious
Excited
Hungry
Eager
Curious
Annoyed
Bored

Unusual Mash-Ups (Fun Bricks)

The more you try the Making It Up Method, the more you'll get used to mixing ideas in unusual ways. One of the joys of improv is the combination of ideas in new and unexpected ways. Try these mashups in any manner you can. Perhaps a character, a location, or even a goal:

Spaghetti factory
Robot daughter
Slinky factory
Spaceship delivery
Castle in the clouds
Underwater barbershop
Moon princess
Unicorn detective
Traveling tree
Jungle skyscraper
Space zoo
Magic broccoli
Nervous desert
Nervous dessert
Laughing mountain
Curious volcano
Loving lava
Money bowl

Opening Lines

I get that the Making It Up technique is different, and starting can be tough. If you can't think of what to say at the beginning of a scene, these lines can help you dive right in. (Note: If you use these once or twice, try NOT using them the following time. These are essentially training wheels for the scene.):

- *Drop the red one!*
- *I can't believe it's raining again.*
- *They're coming, get down!*
- *Welcome to class, please take out your purple book.*
- *It's been a long time, Mom.*
- *This desert air is invigorating.*
- *I ordered my pizza an hour ago.*
- *The castle is smaller than I expected.*
- *At last, we've landed on the moon.*
- *That's it. I quit.*
- *I cannot grant your fourth wish.*
- *Vote for me.*
- *Breathtaking. I'm going to take a photo.*

. . . . .

You've got your tool kit. You've got your rules. You've read through the examples.

By now, you've already started to practice, but you're still only at the beginning of this journey. Every time you try the Making It Up Method, whether it's saying *yes, and* or tapping into an anchor or any other tools, you're growing as a parent, educator, or caregiver. You are building bonds that last, and each time you repeat the method, those bonds will only strengthen. Where will you go with all of this? As far as you can dream.

This is going to be fun.

Notes

CHAPTER 7: MAGIC

1. Marie P. Cross et al., "How and Why Could Smiling Influence Physical Health? A Conceptual Review," *Health Psychology Review* 17, no.2 (2023):321 -343, doi: 10.1080/17437199.2022.2052740.
2. Michalis Drouvelis and Brit Grosskopf, "The Impact of Smiling Cues on Social Cooperation," *South Economic Association* 87, no.4 (January 2021):1390–1404, https://doi.org/10.1002/soej.12485.

CHAPTER 8: ADVENTURES

1. Apologies to anyone familiar with American History or *Star Wars.*

CHAPTER 9: BUMPS

1. This pun was inevitable at some point, given this book's author.
2. Specifically, emotional recall is a component of many modern techniques, but was first codified by Stanislavski in 1906 as a component of what is now referred to as *Method Acting.*

CHAPTER 10: BOUNDARIES

1. Highly overrated.

CHAPTER 11: ONE SIZE DOESN'T FIT ALL

1. Marij Berghs et al., "Drama Therapy for Children and Adolescents with Psychosocial Problems: A Systemic Review on Effects, Means, Therapeutic Attitude, and Supposed Mechanisms of Change," *Children* (Basel) 9, no.9 (September 6, 2022):1358, doi: 10.3390/children9091358.
2. Olivia Rhoades, "Autism Centered Theatre: The Use of Drama to Improve Social Skills for Children on the Autism Spectrum" (master's thesis, EMU, 2014), 866, http://commons.emich.edu/theses/866.

CHAPTER 14: BETTER

1. Talking to you, AI.
2. Vishen Lakhiani, *The Code of the Extraordinary Mind* (Emmaus: Rodale Books, 2019), 19.

CHAPTER 15: ESCAPE

1. There is none. Even if you catch 'em all.

CHAPTER 16: SHOWTIME

1. Jamie Ferri and Greg Hajcak, "Neural Mechanisms Associated with Reappraisal and Attentional Deployment," *Current Opinion Psychology* 3 (June 2015):17-21, doi: 10.1016/j.copsyc.2015.01.010.
2. Heather Wadlinger and Derek M. Isaacowitz, "Fixing Our Focus: Training Attention to Regulate Emotion," *Personality Social Psychology Review* 15, no.1 (February 2011):75-102, doi: 10.1177/1088868310365565.
3. Colás-Blanco, et al., "The Role of Temporal Distance of the Events on the Spatiotemporal Dynamics of Mental Time Travel to One's Personal Past and Future," *Scientific Reports* 12, no. 2378 (February 11, 2022):PAGE , https://doi.org/10.1038/s41598-022-05902-8.
4. Dylan Benkley et al., "Short-Term Implications of Long-Term Thinking: Temporal Distancing and Emotional Responses to Daily Stressors," *Emotion* 23, no. 2 (March 2023):595-599, doi: 10.1037/emo0001140.

Bibliography

Benkley, Dylan, Emily Willroth, Ozlem Ayduk, Oliver John, and Iris B. Mauss. "Short-Term Implications of Long-Term Thinking: Temporal Distancing and Emotional Responses to Daily Stressors." *Emotion* 23, no. 2 (March 2023):595-599. doi: 10.1037/emo0001140.

Berghs, Marij, Anna-Eva J. C. Prick, Constance Vissers, Susan van Hooren. "Drama Therapy for Children and Adolescents with Psychosocial Problems: A Systemic Review on Effects, Means, Therapeutic Attitude, and Supposed Mechanisms of Change." *Children (Basel) 9, no.9* (September 6, 2022):1358. doi: 10.3390/children9091358.

Colás-Blanco, J. Mioche, V. La Corte, and P. Piolino. "The Role of Temporal Distance of the Events on the Spatiotemporal Dynamics of Mental Time Travel to One's Personal Past and Future." *Scientific Reports* 12, no. 2378 (February 11, 2022):PAGE . https://doi.org/10.1038/s41598-022-05902-8.

Cross, Marie P., Amanda M. Acevedo, Kate A. Leger, and Sarah D. Pressman. "How and Why Could Smiling Influence Physical Health? A Conceptual Review." *Health Psychology Review* 17, no.2 (2023):321-343. doi: 10.1080/17437199.2022.2052740.

Drouvelis, Michalis, and Brit Grosskopf. "The Impact of Smiling Cues on Social Cooperation." *South Economic Association* 87, no.4 (January 2021):1390–1404. https://doi.org/10.1002/soej.12485.

Ferri, Jamie, and Greg Hajcak. "Neural Mechanisms Associated with Reappraisal and Attentional Deployment." *Current Opinion Psychology* 3 (June 2015):17-21. doi: 10.1016/j.copsyc.2015.01.010.

Lakhiani, Vishen. *The Code of the Extraordinary Mind*. Emmaus: Rodale Books, 2019).

Rhoades, Olivia. "Autism Centered Theatre: The Use of Drama to Improve Social Skills for Children on the Autism Spectrum." Master's thesis, EMU, 2014. 866.http://commons.emich.edu/theses/866.

Wadlinger, Heather, and Derek M. Isaacowitz. "Fixing Our Focus: Training Attention to Regulate Emotion." *Personality Social Psychology Review* 15, no.1 (February 2011):75-102. doi: 10.1177/1088868310365565.

ABOUT THE CREATORS

CHRISTOPHER MANNINO began his writing journey after becoming stranded on a cliff in Cornwall, at the legendary birthplace of King Arthur. He watched the sunrise over castle ruins and was inspired to write *The Scythe Wielder's Secret*. Since then, he's written thirty books. He is one of Business Insider's most read writers with over 4.5m readers. Before leaving teaching to raise his children as a stay-at-home dad, he was a theatre teacher and improvisation coach. Visit him at www.ChristopherMannino.com

CORY REID has a BA Honors Degree in Illustration from Loughborough University and has a passion for creating adorable characters and worlds for them to inhabit. His charming digital style features fine detailing and is beautifully textured. Cory has worked in the creative industry for almost twenty years, starting as a greeting card designer before moving into publishing. He has already had several titles published for clients including Usborne Publishing, Owlet Press, Autumn Publishing, and Pan Macmillan.

ABOUT FAMILIUS

Visit Our Website: www.familius.com

Familius is a global trade publishing company that publishes books and other content to help families be happy. We believe that happy families are key to a better society and the foundation of a happy life. The greatest work anyone will ever do will be within the walls of his or her own home. And we don't mean vacuuming! We recognize that every family looks different and passionately believe in helping all families find greater joy, whatever their situation. To that end, we publish beautiful books that help families live our 10 Habits of Happy Family Life: *love together, play together, learn together, work together, talk together, heal together, read together, eat together, give together,* and *laugh together*. Further, Familius does not discriminate on the basis of race, color, religion, gender, age, nationality, disability, caste, or sexual orientation in any of its activities or operations. Founded in 2012, Familius is located in Sanger, California.

Connect

- Facebook: www.facebook.com/familiusbooks
- Pinterest: www.pinterest.com/familiusbooks
- Instagram: @FamiliusBooks
- TikTok: @FamiliusBooks

FAMILIUS

THE MOST IMPORTANT WORK YOU EVER DO WILL BE WITHIN THE WALLS OF YOUR OWN HOME.